Happ,

Lori Peters

Getting Married at Last

My Journey from Hopelessness to Happiness

Getting Married at Last

My Journey from Hopelessness to Happiness

Lori A. Peters

Ride along with me on my winding, tumultuous journey to find my true self and ultimate happiness. You'll meet my memorable passengers—the most challenging, impactful love relationships I've experienced—and probably recognize some of your own along the way. My hope is that you find inspiration and confidence as you reflect on your own life, especially if you have given up on love, are starting over, or want to take your relationship to the next level.

Lori A. Peters, Author

Together We Win Publishing, Publisher
www.happinesshangout.net • happyhangout@gmail.com

This publication has been compiled based on personal experience, research, and anecdotal evidence, but is not intended to replace legal, financial, or other professional advice or services. Every reasonable attempt has been made to provide accurate content, and the author and publisher disclaim responsibility for any errors or omissions contained herein. The samples provided are for educational and discussion purposes only. All website addresses cited were current at the time of publication. Any trademarks, service marks, product names, or named features are assumed to be the property of their respective owners and are used solely for editorial reference, not endorsement.

Published in the United States of America, 2017

ISBN-13: 978-0-9989049-1-7 (E-book)

ISBN-13: 978-0-9989049-0-0 (Paperback)

Dedication

This book is dedicated to my parents, James and Barbara Peters. I thank them with all my heart for providing me a solid foundation so I could finally soar in life when I was ready.

Acknowledgments

I must first thank my husband, Ryan. Without him, I would have not been able to finish this book, and this dream would not have become a reality. He is the anchor in my support system, as he loves me truly for who I am, crazy personality and all.

My book team is a force to be reckoned with. Thank you to BNI (Core Connection Chapter of Business Networking International, Medina, Ohio) for bringing me my editor and writing coach, Gail Kerzner. Her compassion, wit, and thoughtfulness, along with her keen eye and knowledge, kept me from losing my mind in a world in which I was new. Thank you to Gail for bringing me Donna Duchek, who started out as my cover designer but ended up being so much more: technical, marketing and book sales advisor.

Thank you to the staff at *Your Tango*, who believed in my work and introduced me to numerous professionals who all support each other in our passion of helping others. Special thanks to Melanie Gorman, who spent time helping me understand my brand and how to start the book writing process.

Much gratitude to Happiness Hangout® supporters, friends, family, numerous others who I connect with every day on social media, my radio show guests, listeners, and especially my book tribe, who help each other bring our work to the world.

Contents

Dedication   *v*

Acknowledgments   *vi*

Contents   *viii*

Introduction   *xiii*

CHAPTER 1

Pullin' Out of the Station—   *1*

the Journey Begins

    Welcome to My Weirdness

    How Family Shaped Me, Whether I Liked It or Not

    Role Models Are Not Perfect — And That's Okay

CHAPTER 2

The Little Caboose   *15*

Chugs Through Her Relationships

    My Jaded and Messed Up Thinking

CHAPTER 3

Going Down the Wrong Side of the Track   *21*

    The Sacred Land of Youth — I Don't Know Nothin'

Are You Kidding Me?

Come On, Girl—Open Your Heart

CHAPTER 4

Letting Off Steam   *31*

While Trying to Stay on the Rails

College—Now That's Where the Boys Are

The College Balancing Act—

I'm an Adult, Kind Of

Two Different Tracks

The Agony of Dancing

on the Party Train

The Uncatchable Fish

The Lasting Lesson I Now Know

CHAPTER 5

Chugging Along   *45*

to the Next Stations

The Girl Becomes a Woman—Finally

Stepping Forward and Moving Back Again

The Real Grad School Lessons

CHAPTER 6

Ugh, I Keep Missing the Marriage Stop *55*

I'm Not Really a Loser, Am I?

Keep Stroking That Ego

A New Career and New Men

CHAPTER 7

The Unthinkable Happens: *65*
A Tragic Derailment

Could It Get Worse Than This? Nope!

The Train Derailed and Came

to a Screeching Halt...

Moment of Revelation

CHAPTER 8

All Aboard! Moving Along Again   *71*
in the Right Direction

New Beginnings

The Right Direction Detour

Revving Up the Engine Again

A Breakthrough Revelation

CHAPTER 9

Stopping at the Depot   *80*
for a Breather

Alone in the Full Swing of Life

Hibernating to Heal

My Surprise Seatmate

Teachers Can Sometimes Have Four Legs

Starting to Come Alive Again

A Moment of Clarity

CHAPTER 10

Onward Again: The Glimmer   *97*
at the End of the Tunnel

Practicing What I Preach

Taking Myself to the Next Level — The Epiphany

Moment of Reflection

Living Life to the Fullest

CHAPTER 11

Finally — The Love Train   *104*
Arrives at the Depot

A Relationship in the Making

Love Is Here, and I'm Ready

Moment of Clarity

Let's Celebrate!

CHAPTER 12

Keeping My Relationship   *116*
on Track

The Journey Continues

Managing the Unexpected

Overcoming Boredom

You Spoiled, Rotten Brat

Choosing the Light Side

THE AFTERSTORY

Relationship Advice   *126*

from the Passenger on the Train

It All Starts with You

Balance Is the Key to Life

Compassion Shows Strength

Gratitude Is Life Changing

What If Your Beloved Isn't Showing Up?

Don't Ever Give Up

What Does It Mean to Be Happy?

About the Author   *139*

Resources   *141*

The Happiness Hangout®   *143*

Testimonials   *145*

Gratitude Journal Information   *149*

Happiness Hangout® **Blogs**   *154*

Introduction

All aboard! Ride along with me on my winding, tumultuous journey from hopelessness to happiness as the love train pulls out of the station in high school, meanders in and out of hills and valleys, veers off the track, and then comes to a screeching halt — for days, months, and yes, even years.

You'll meet my memorable passengers, the most challenging, impactful love relationships I've experienced, and probably recognize some of your own along the way.

Slowly, but surely, I force myself to buy a ticket for a different route, leave my worn baggage behind, and climb aboard for more adventures. I chug along, experiencing good, bad, and ugly relationships until my *aha moment* appears, I evolve into my true self, and find *the one.* Although it took decades for me to become my true self, I explain how I got through it and came out on the other side.

Let your own emotions go, as I retell stories of relationships through crocodile tears as well as my irreverent but endearing sense of humor. I sometimes found myself laughing so hard at my own memories, I had to change my clothes.

My former love interests' names have been changed "to protect the innocent" (or not so innocent). Moving through this life, I realized that my ex-boyfriends and I were just doing the best we could; we all just needed room to grow. None of us could claim we were perfect. We were just all trying to make our way in life, sloppy and disturbing as much of it was.

I decided to write this book after my struggles with *finding* love were over. I also wrote my story to inspire others to realize that they can find the relationship of their lives as well. It doesn't matter if you're twenty-seven or seventy. If you're in the right headspace, you can and will find your partner. You may even learn more about your life than you imagined.

Remember that love takes many forms — love of self, parents, friends and family, and relationships with our animal companions. I knew I wanted love in a partner, but that doesn't mean that is a goal for every human being. Happiness is defined uniquely for each person. The lessons I learned on my journey apply to all kinds of relationships.

I hope my transformation awakens you to new possibilities. Life is too short to give up on yourself, the relationship of your dreams, or anything else you want for that matter. I felt compelled to not only share my challenging, impactful journey with you but also to provide inspiration and opportunities for deeper reflection so you may live your life with more confidence and peace.

Let this book be a source of light, hope, and the spark that reminds you that you can have beautiful, loving relationships, no matter what path in life you are on.

Getting Married at Last

My Journey from Hopelessness to Happiness

Lori A. Peters

CHAPTER 1

Pullin' Out of the Station— the Journey Begins

"H-h-hi," I whimpered. "It's over, and he's gone. I can't believe this is happening—again!" My best friend, Melissa, asked me what happened, and as I have so many times before, I tell her the story. It's the same tale I always tell, just with a different guy at a different time. Another love lost.

This scenario is called "my pattern"—doing the same thing over and over again and having no idea how to stop it. This pattern started when I was young, as many do.

Welcome to My Weirdness

Awkward, uncomfortable, and unworthy: These are the

feelings I remember about my childhood. Can you say "low self-esteem?" Yes, you can, and you should because this nine-year-old was not having fun. From the time I was conscious of my surroundings, I knew I wasn't pretty. I remember looking in the mirror making that ugly face, somehow knowing that I was describing myself. I had thin, scraggly, mousey-brown hair, an overbite, and a nose that seemed to cover my face like I was some kind of female Jimmy Durante. (The comedian made his living by joking about his nose.)

At the time, I thought that I inherited all the worst physical features from my parents. I had my mom's absurdly big toe from who knows where. We are not aware of any other relative owning this precious gem. I didn't get my mom's big boobs until much later, and my hips sunk battleships. Individually, my dad and mom had fine noses and eyes, but in my opinion, the combination that appeared on my face didn't look right. Too bad I never noticed what was attractive about my looks back then. That came years later. To top it off, I displayed a foul mood that was the product of my anger — anger at the world, God, and my family for not making me pretty.

There is no way that attitude was going to translate well into the world. And boy, it didn't. Add to that my people-pleasing ways, and we had a recipe for sadness and heartbreak. Oh, and one more thing: I got my period at 9! Actually, I was almost 10. Becoming a woman *technically* at 10 is not a confidence builder. It felt bizarre to say the least, as most 10-year-olds *do not* know how to process this. I just woke up one morning, looked in the toilet, and screamed, "MOM!" She was calm and collected, while I was freaking out. That was our usual communication method throughout our lives. My first question to her was, "Do I bleed like this every day for the rest of my life?" She laughed and assured me it was only one week out of every four. *OMG . What?* I was bleeding through my vagina at barely ten years old! I was traumatized but went to school that day, cramps and all. I could not concentrate, and when Mrs. Roman called on me to answer a math question, I thought, "Are you kidding lady? I'm dying here!" Mom and I never discussed menstrual cycles because — well — I was a child. I guess she thought we had a few more years.

How Family Shaped Me,
Whether I Liked It or Not

I was the apple of my mother's eye. We had similar faces and personalities, and her world revolved around me. Thank goodness, because this self-proclaimed, awkward mess of a kid needed her support badly. She was 5'6" with bristly, brown hair that looked like she walked successfully through a windstorm. She had it *done* every week like most ladies from the Silent Generation, and it drooped in two days. Her "poop-brown eyes" (as she referred to them) showed her cunning wit. Her tongue was so sharp, it cut people into shreds if they got on her bad side. The most intimidating women I knew told me my mother terrified them. If she liked you, she treated you like gold. If she didn't, watch out! Once we went to a neighbor's party, and this friend of a friend and she got into it about some dumb thing, and I watched my mom go at him like a shark tangling with its bait. That guy never knew what hit him, as mom verbally slammed him as she snidely sipped her black coffee. Dad just sat back and enjoyed the show, as I ran back to my house to avoid confrontation.

The good news is she loved to have fun and laughed at my silly antics. My parents used to play a Cheech and Chong album after hours at our Dairy Queen business, and I would imitate the filthy-mouthed 1970s comedians. She kept trying to turn down the volume when they dropped the F-Bomb, which was about every five seconds. I was nine, and I told her to give it up already. She said, "No way!" But eventually, I talked her into continuing to let the album roll. I usually got what I wanted if I wanted it badly enough. I was even respectful enough to skip all the F words during my comedy show. I figured I'd wait until I was at least ten before I moved into the adult version. On my eleventh birthday, I begged and pleaded for a cherry red Le Tour 10-speed bike. My parents said it was too much money and that I'd hardly ride it. I am a salesperson at heart, so I used every tactic in the book: made my case for exercising, having fun with friends, and getting more fresh air. They were having none of it — until the bike showed up in the garage. Lori: 1 Parents: 0!

My dad was quite the character. He was a *guy's guy* but quiet, sweet, and kind. He was a 6-foot tall, handsome man with bright green eyes. In my parents' wedding pictures, he looked like Buddy Holly with his wavy, dark hair and black, square-rimmed glasses. Dad was *go with the flow,* to put it mildly, and the man was *always* late, as he sang to his own tune. As my mother put it, "When you were ziggin', he was zaggin'." While the neighborhood was in peaceful slumber, he was snow blowing the driveway at 3 a.m. Nobody even knew what a snow blower was in 1976, but we had one. Dad was an early adopter, as they say in marketing, and we were the first to have many conveniences, such as central air conditioning. Yes, he figured out how to find one, install it himself, and maintain it for many years. We also had a microwave and satellite TV that my Dad rigged up years before anyone else had them. He used to go to what I called "the Star Trek room" into the spare closet, go up through the ceiling, do something mysterious, and — voila! — hundreds of channels from some alien place would appear on our TV.

Needless to say, my friends liked hanging out at my house because my dad's hobby was stereo sound systems. He had 32 speakers in the basement and cranked out jazz, blues, Led Zeppelin, Creedence Clearwater Revival, and so much more like we were at a live show at Madison Square

Garden. He soundproofed the basement with sand, which poured out of the walls for the next thirty years. My mom almost tumbled off her chair when The Audio Warehouse retail store sent my dad a Christmas card in 1977. That kind of marketing was not prevalent back then, so you know old Shumbo (That was his nickname my friend came up with out of the blue.) spent a lot of cash there.

My parents were both old school — work hard, play later kind of people. They didn't believe in building self-esteem, and they expected me to be humble. But this child needed compliments so desperately. I had little to no belief in myself, and this lack of confidence came from a place inside me. No one was mean or abusive to me, and I had no one to blame. I just didn't like how I looked in the mirror. When I was about 13, my dad and I were joking around, and I ended up sitting on his lap in the kitchen. My mom was making dinner and said, "You look like you're gaining weight again." Her comment triggered me to ask, "Why don't you ever say anything nice about me?" She turned around, looking shocked and sad. She told me that her family never gave many accolades because they thought their children might turn out to be egotistical.

I knew Mom loved me by her actions, not her words.
I told her that it would be helpful if she complimented
me once in a while. For the first time in my life, I saw my
mom vulnerable. She apologized and said that it was hard
for her, but she would try. As usual, my dad just sat there
not saying anything. I'm not sure if he was just taking it
all in or if he didn't hear most of it. He was actually born
70% deaf.

Because of the combination of my internal angst
about my looks and my inherited anxious and somewhat
depressed nature, I needed lots of extra support. Although
I am grateful for the way my wonderful parents raised
me, I certainly could have used a therapist while I was
growing up to provide me with the coping skills that my
parents just didn't have to share.

Mom always told me Dad was an extremely sensitive
man, but you couldn't tell. He didn't often show his
feelings. Once he said, "I hate emotions," which revealed a
lot about his psychological well-being as well as the irony
that his statement was, in fact, emotional. He never talked
about feelings, but he did show me affection — thank
goodness. He hugged me often, and I could sense how

much he loved being around me by the warmth that emanated from him onto me. He wasn't dead inside by a long shot, but his heart and soul could have used some reviving. That can happen when you have a tumultuous upbringing like he did.

When he was eight years old, my grandmother sent him to live in foster care for a few years. She just could not handle the stress of life, as she was only sixteen when she gave birth to him. My paternal grandfather was out of the scene, and Grandma ended up marrying another man and having a few more kids. My dad's sister revealed that he was relieved to be away from the chaos, and his foster family saved his life because they taught him discipline and structure. By the time he got back home, Grandma's husband had died. Dad was much older than his siblings and had to take on the father role. They were poor, and my dad quit school to work at our town's small grocery store when he was around fourteen. He worked all day and into the evening and came home to unruly brothers and sisters who were doing their best to help out. It baffles me that he turned out to be even remotely normal. All he wanted was to find a swell girl to marry with a stable family.

And that he found. Miracles do happen.

Every night, Dad would sit down and try to talk with me about whatever was going on in my life. When I was a teenager, I blew that off because I was a bitch who didn't understand what was happening to me when I was maturing. I was moodier than a Kardashian on a diet. He would tease me so I would interact with him. He would wrap his index finger and thumb around my knee and squeeze. Yikes! That got my attention. We would joke around and play *fight*. I know I hurt his feelings so many times with my crappy attitude. I was there physically but not mentally. I would just look at him and blow him off with my eyes. I hope I made it up to him by becoming a good person later in life who treated him with respect and care. I thought the world of my dad. Considering his upbringing, I believe his ability to show love on any level was an amazing feat.

I think dads should be a big deal in young girls' lives. And my dad was certainly a big deal in my life. They teach us how men should treat us. They show us what we can expect from relationships, and their impact on us is profound. Our parents' love for each other, or lack thereof, is our first encounter with this type of union.

It can — and usually does — affect us for many years, or maybe our entire lives.

Role Models Are Not Perfect—And That's Okay

My parents' love for each other was evident until I was about 10. Before that, I saw them kissing, and I think I heard them say "I love you" to each other a few times. Then something happened that I didn't understand for years. They became complacent — just like that. They used to argue and make *fun* bets with each other. For example, on Saturday nights, the dictionary came out because they were having a debate and betting money on word definitions. It was like watching *Revenge Of The Nerds* — Peters' style. Then the love just seemed to . . . stop. They began to merely co-exist in the same house. Communication breakdown evolved into just going through the motions. Yes, it was much more peaceful, but I felt like they gave up. They almost got divorced, and my mom was preparing to move us in with her mother.

Then one night, I heard them in their bedroom down the hall. My mom was sobbing and talking, and I didn't hear a peep out of my dad. I think this went on for an hour or two. My mom came into my bedroom in the middle of the night, hugged me, and said, "It's going to be okay, honey. It's going to be okay." The next morning, I abruptly pulled out the "For Sale" sign and threw it across the front yard. And that was it. My parents began their journey of loneliness together for the next 24 years — all for me. I'm sure of it.

As sad as my parents' relationship seemed, we did have fun and laughed a lot, even though they were always stressed about running their Dairy Queen. I didn't realize Mom and Dad's relationship was my model of normalcy. I viewed love and marriage as two people managing to get along in life without much affection or attention to each other. They still spent time together going out to dinner every Saturday and visiting friends, but the message I got was, "Let's just trudge along." This behavior may not have been reality, but I perceived it that way, so much so that my romantic relationships often had many of the same traits. I just never noticed the similarity, and it took me years to realize it. I pulled away from men if I sensed even the slightest thing was going wrong. Maybe the man of the hour didn't call that day, or perhaps he didn't mention when I'd be seeing him again. I perceived almost everything happening with a negative slant, and I'd begin to shut down mentally. Communication breakdown at its best.

As it turned out, my dad's true colors — loyalty and consideration — came out years later when my mom began to get sick. She tried so hard but could not stop smoking, which lead to problems like carotid arteries, heart issues, and eventually strokes. My dad made sure he was at all of her doctors' appointments and catered to her needs after she had a surgery. Dad wasn't outwardly loving; he showed care in the way he worked so hard to keep us financially stable and his constant teasing of us. Frankly, seeing him being overtly nurturing was refreshing and generally made me feel less anxious about Mom's illnesses. I didn't feel alone watching her suffer because I now had a compadre in the experience. Once she was feeling better, my mom said something like, "You know, your dad knows how to come through when he needs to. I can't imagine being married to anyone but your father." "Wow!" I thought. "Really? Well, good then." I watched them, and they utterly confused me. On the one hand, they didn't seem to be a connected couple. On the other hand, they seemed to be making it. This just shows that situations aren't always as they seem, and relationships can be complicated. I realize now how my parents shaped my life and my love relationships. If only I had seen that years ago. As a maturing person with her own insecurities, I could only process a limited amount of information. I knew they were good people, loved me, and deeply cared about my needs and wants. What I did not see was their outward love for each other. I saw their marriage as a structured, daily routine instead of a tightly-bonded relationship that demonstrated tender moments. As a kid, I needed to see that.

I realized that my parents' relationship was full of flaws. So what did I do as I explored my own love life as a young person? Who did I look to for guidance and advice? How did I know if I was doing it right?

I looked towards my friends, of course.

CHAPTER 2

The Little Caboose Chugs Through Her Relationships

My Jaded and Messed Up Thinking

I met my tribe in junior high school. Those years can be so awkward, and I was the queen of awkward. I had a mature body: I had a 5' 7" frame, wore a B cup bra and respectable, size-nine pants. I had no idea what to do with that body, my mind, or life in general. Looking back on it, I believe my friends, in contrast, had their shit together, considering they were so young. They were all smart, levelheaded young people that had their own dreams and goals. Thank heavens, because that solid support group made all the difference when I was in my early teens. None of them

15

was sleazy or gossiped incessantly. They all had their own boyfriend patterns, and I could have learned a thing or two from them, but I didn't. I buried myself in my own muck, too immature to open my eyes and let a little light shine in. They allowed boys to hang out with them, go steady, and canoodle at basketball games — typical middle school behavior.

As most young teens do, I appointed my friends as my advisors. This may be good or bad depending on who your friends are. How *together* were my friends? Did they have my best interests at heart? Yes, they did. Were they mature and wise enough to help me through the hurdles? Probably not, but the smartest thing for me was just to listen. I wasn't smart in that sense, though, and could not do that. I was an extroverted leader who loved to give advice, so I was screwed.

I loved to hear myself talk, and I thought I could cure all that ailed everyone, even though I had absolutely no idea what I was talking about. My early experiences with boys were a disaster most of the time, yet I had all the answers, and many of my friends thought they did too.

Some of my favorite responses from well-meaning

school buds about my love relationships were: "Why would he do that to you?" They'd say, "He'll be back," or "He's a loser." I've got tons more excuses and some swampland in Florida I can sell you. And by the way, why was there all this thinking and running away? Eighth-grade boys *do not* think that much.

Within my tribe, I had two best friends. Jessica and I met the first day of seventh grade, and she *always* had a boyfriend. She had that *it* factor that was hard to explain, that *I'm girlfriend material* vibe that boys picked up on. I have no idea how she did it, but she did. Jessica always loved having a boyfriend, and they loved having her. When one relationship ended, she'd have another guy in line waiting. Even with all these suitors, we were with each other 24/7, yet her dating pattern didn't rub off on me. Once, a guy even broke up with her! She didn't know what to do. She followed me around for days because she just needed somebody to hold on to mentally and physically. She asked me if this was okay, and I said, "Absolutely." I felt so good to be able to help her. Jessica recovered pretty quickly and moved on to the next one — and her relationship pattern continued until she married.

My other bestie was the prom queen — not literally, but she could have been. Lisa was stunning, and the guys loved her. Her dark gold, Farah Fawcett-feathered hair swayed in the wind as her emerald eyes twinkled. She had a perfect smile and a shapely, attractive figure which was on its way to becoming an eye-popping, *hot* body. *Bitch* — just kidding! We met in 6th grade, and I knew then that we needed to be friends. It's so strange how you know you need someone in your life, but you aren't conscious of the reason. If she's got the boys, by extension of our friendship, I would too. What a bonus!

Two boys used to hang out at my house after school. I lived in a middle-class neighborhood in a lovely, two-story, four-bedroom house with a spacious yard. My parents gave me everything I could want. They were generous to others too, especially when it came to food and sharing treats from our Dairy Queen. I don't believe Steven and Bill hung out with us for the treats; I think their middle school hormones were raging. Steven really liked Lisa; Bill either liked her too or was just looking for something to do. After spending time with them for several weeks, Lisa told me Bill was kind of *into me.*

I remember loving this comment, but nothing came of it. This experience happened enough times that if I had mustered just a bit more gumption, life could have been different then. If I had been more self-assured, or at least if I could have talked to someone about how I was feeling, perhaps I would have been able to raise my low self-esteem. I often wonder why I didn't just go to my mom and tell her about all this, but I was embarrassed. I didn't want anyone to know how I felt about myself. I was an oversensitive person and got my feelings hurt so easily as a kid. I had zero backbone at the time and had no idea how to get some of it. I wanted it so badly.

The good news was I got good grades and used my leadership skills to help plan eighth-grade school choir events and organize my friends' weekly fall Friday night football games. Here's how it went: you wore your cutest outfit, which in 1978 was a pair of trendy denim overalls with a colorful blouse and your Earth Shoes. If you were stylin', you pranced around in some beige suede, four-inch platforms. You threw in your denim jacket on top of your denim outfit, and you're in for a jeans jubilee like none other. Then all of us ladies proceeded to walk the football stadium for three hours talking to boys. Round and round we went until it was over. We explored life's issues like who was making out under the stands. Who got together and broke up? Which boys were acting like jerks? Should we apply more lip gloss or not? Once our football shenanigans ended, we were starving, and it was pizza time. Then we moved on to a sleepover, where we continued our discussions about boys and our hair. Ah, the good old days.

I worked desperately to cover my major flaws through my friends. I wasn't aware of it yet, but if confident, beautiful people were around me, I could then be connected to their qualities by default. I masked my greatness by standing in the background and hoping others' light would shine onto me instead of seeking out my own brightness.

I could tag along and at least be part of the thrill of it all, but I was still locked away from *living* my beauty and confidence and would continue in this vein for a *long* time.

CHAPTER 3

Going Down the Wrong Side of the Track

The Sacred Land of Youth— I Don't Know Nothin'

High school was a wonderful experience — *not*. I was a teenager who was a bit chunky but not fat and had some fashion sense, but I was dealing with some sinus issues that made me feel self-conscious: the constant drainage, the disgusting taste, and my nervous stomach to boot. I'm glad I didn't need to write an online dating profile in high school because it would have sounded *less* than appealing: "Nervous high school girl, kind of not fat, occasionally cute but with poor self-esteem, sinus problems, and acidy stomach seeks self-confident, college-bound, football-lettered male with a sweet, kind, giving personality that looks like a 1980s Donny Osmond." Apparently, I enjoyed setting myself up for rejection because that's the kind of boy I wanted, but so did all the girls. And what chance did I have?

My insecurities raged. Imagine going into a massive high school environment of close to three thousand students. I thought my teachers, the guidance counselor, or the principal might help me navigate this overwhelming storm, but they were less than helpful, so I had to tap into my tribe and latch on for the four-year ride.

I know I had some fun in high school. I just don't remember much of it. I do remember the embarrassing stuff that stuck to me like glue. Inheriting the sensitive gene from my dad, I took to heart any negativity launched toward me.

Oh, the joy of the infamous high school parties: AKA make out time. At one Friday night party, I was kissing this boy, and all seemed fine. I even fanaticized that maybe he liked me, and I would see what happened at school on Monday. A few days went by, and I heard this rumor: "Lori Peters kisses like a walrus!" First of all, how does he know how a walrus kisses? And if he does know, that's gross — and a good rumor-starter too.

I could not think straight. My head was spinning with thoughts of the most popular kids teasing me in the hallways. What would my friends say? Maybe I'd never have a peaceful day at school again! Naturally, some immature football player in my English class made fun of me about it. Tracy (Yes, I could have teased him about his name, but I controlled myself.) was telling the story not to just a few people but also to anyone in the class who would listen. If shitting a brick had been possible, my butt would have built a three-bedroom condo that day.

Surprisingly, I had the guts to go to a principal and tell him that I was having trouble. Of course, I did not give him any details. I just admitted that this kid in class was constantly bothering me and that I could not concentrate. He asked me what happened. How was I going to tell this story to an adult? Was he going to call my parents? My mother would have cracked up laughing and then yelled at me for making out with this boy. I'd never be able to look any school administrator in the eyes again for the next 2+ years. *No way!* My lips were sealed, unlike the previous

Friday night. Since I wasn't talking, he basically told me to suck it up.

I can only imagine if we had used social media back then. I can see it now: Instagram pics of my face attached to a walrus' body being sent around to my schoolmates. I'm so glad I grew up in the dark ages of the 80s. My ego says that I had skills in French kissing, and he didn't — so I'm going with that. After all, you've gotta move that tongue around a little, right? Just like a walrus' mouth moves around. My 52-year-old self looks back and laughs. My 15-year-old self wanted to die.

Some boys bothered me about it for several months with their walrus imitations. They made that horrible walrus noise and flapped their hands together when I walked by. That is *not* what I needed. I'm sure I was a complete sucker, as the pain showed all over my face. Of course, that pain drives bullying even further. My daydream used to be that I turned around, looked them in the eyes, and retorted, "You're ignorant and rude, and most of the girls don't like you. And I should know because they *all* tell me so!" Then they would humbly escape, hunched over, holding their tiny penises between their legs.

Oh, how I wish I'd had my mom's tenacity when I was a teenager. I would have had some fun messing with those little testosterone-driven minions. That one moment of internal strength pouring out of me and the tiny white lie I told could have gone a long way in opening my path toward self-love. But I didn't have the gumption yet. And I had more significant, unnerving issues waiting for me ahead.

Are You Kidding Me?

My mom decided that tenth grade was the right time to discuss teenage pregnancy — my *potential* teenage pregnancy. Although my girlfriends and I had talked a lot about sex, we never thought through what would happen if we really *got* pregnant. That's because none of us was having sex yet. At least that's what they all told me. Fortunately, I remained a virgin in high school because I was not ready for anything beyond kissing with my confidence level at an all-time low.

Mom and I were sitting on the front porch stoop, and out of nowhere, she said, "You know, Lori, if you ever accidentally got pregnant, we'll just take care of it." Holy hell! I almost passed out! My Catholic mother was obviously pro-choice, but this was shocking to me. She wanted me to have the best life I could, and she wasn't letting *anything* get in the way.

All of a sudden, I had a new fear — *sex*. There was no way I was going to get myself into trouble. I would disappoint my parents beyond belief, and supposedly, she'd want me to have an abortion. I wanted no part of any of it. To this day, I don't know if she was trying to scare me to death or meant what she said.

But there was this one boy my junior year. He sought me out and made it clear he wanted to date me. He told all my friends and cautiously flirted every minute he was around me. I wasn't sure if I was being punked or what. I wasn't used to this treatment and attention from boys. Justin was so adorable with his short, thick, straight, dirty, dishwater-brown hair and his husky six-foot physique. I loved his squinty, bright blue eyes and radiant smile. His skin was a silky, soft, naturally tan color, yet he was so rugged. He wore flannel shirts, and his jeans hung on him because he didn't have much of a butt. He had the best sense of humor on the planet. We called him Pit Boy because he could spit watermelon seeds to extraordinary lengths and make jokes while he did it. He imitated our classmates and voices of movie stars like Clint Eastwood and Sylvester Stallone. He did an admirable Mick Jagger and Bon Scott from AC/DC too. He smiled all the time, complimented me often, and treated me so nicely. He was a bit shy when it came to the girls, but Justin asked me out on dates, and we hung out at the mall. What else do high schoolers do?

I could tell back then that he was *relationship material* and wanted to spend time with me. What a sweet soul! We were both 16, but that was the only major similarity between us. I liked jocks, and he wasn't one. He just lugged himself around like a slow-moving locomotive — chugga chug, choo choo. I mean that in the nicest way possible, by the way. He went to vocational school and studied auto mechanics, and I was college bound. That was enough for me not to give him a chance, even though I remember going out to eat with him and holding hands. I was so conflicted because I did like him, but my low self-esteem was never going to allow it. So I put on my big, bad attitude, masked myself as a brat, and decided that if he wasn't college material, then Justin wasn't for me. I was never going to admit that I was too terrified to move even an inch forward with him. Bye bye, Pit Boy.

Come On, Girl—Open Your Heart

I feel horrible for the few boys I did blow off. I hate the thought that I might have given them a complex, like they weren't good enough when truly the problem was *me*. I do know that I had to forgive myself for being such a jerk. I was a young girl, and my brain wasn't anywhere near fully developed. I'm sorry for me and what could have been, yet I am aware that certain experiences can only happen in their own time. That was not the time — not yet.

To this day I dream about high school. I'm often running through hallways, up and down school stairs trying to get to my classroom that I can't find. Or I have to take a test and didn't study for it at all, and I'm terrified of failing. Oops, that may have happened a time or two. It's the classic insecurity/fear dream. Unresolved issues abound, and I was pushing them down.

I really didn't want to put much energy into thinking about high school. I had moved on mentally, and there was no need to revisit it. But then came social media.

I finally gave in and started connecting online with my Class of 1982 Austintown Fitch High School Facebook group. I think curiosity got the best of me, and I decided to let go of my rigid decisions about the past and maybe get to know my schoolmates in the present. Maybe I would be able to replace old memories of immature kids with new memories of some nice adults. We didn't have any reunions because most of us didn't seem interested, but a few in our online group claim that we are now the best class in school history. We communicate with each other, meet up more than once a year, and one member posts when both tragic and miraculous things happen to us. Pretty amazing. Funny how perspective and time can change everything. Who knows? Maybe we are one of the best.

Why do we proclaim that we will *never, ever* do something, and after fighting it to the nth degree, we do it? Because people, circumstances, and situations *do* change. Trying to stay open minded and allowing the seemingly impossible even to be probable allowed me to explore my uncomfortable high school years. Friendships and even deep relationships that seemed totally out of reach could end up developing. By living life, I constantly find myself in circumstances that surprise me. It could happen to you too. And my friends, that's a good thing.

CHAPTER 4

Letting Off Steam While Trying to Stay on the Rails

College—Now That's Where the Boys Are

For many traditionally-aged, college-bound females, the university setting includes a plethora of eligible men. The jump from high school to college was exhilarating, a rite of passage that affected me like nothing else had previously. Everything happened at warp speed. I joined a sorority my first quarter which, to this day, was one of my best moves. I launched into the only real social scene at Youngstown State University, took advantage of valuable leadership opportunities, and gained training and skills for future employment. I needed a lifeline to the social scene too. My tribe had now increased tenfold, and they were there for me.

I now had others, more knowledgeable than I, to show me the ropes. I wanted to meet all kinds of people, especially men, and I did. Mixers, football games, parties — all the action came at me like a high-speed locomotive. I was reeling from the possibilities, but I also brought along some of the old high school baggage. I took a major leap of growth, at least allowing myself to have a relationship. One of my sorority sisters introduced me to my first, true boyfriend within my first few months of college.

Mike was a fraternity man. He was sweet, handsome, and Italian, with dark hair and a 1983 moustache — which was *cool* at the time, I think. We met at a mixer at his fraternity house and hit it off right away. He was a senior and getting ready to graduate, and I was a lowly freshman. I was attracted to his maturity and fun-loving nature. We went on actual dates! We dated for about three months, and it went pretty darn well. We hung out at YSU events together and went to upscale restaurants. I felt all tingly inside to be wined and dined; I was not used to this kind of treatment. I dressed up in my padded-shoulder sweater, black knee-length skirt, and my essential Barracuda jacket. Having cocktails in the heart of Youngstown's most notable Italian cuisine wasn't foreign to me, but in a dating situation, I was in another world. I enjoyed being on his arm at other sorority events too, because for the first time, I felt like I had a man of my own. Then we broke up just like that — poof — done. I have no idea why. It just ended; we just stopped communicating. No fretting, no crying, no drama. All I know is he was one of the first young men that I didn't freak out over losing. Ordinarily, I'd be preparing to shut myself down, dreaming of when we'd get back together and launching into a wave of sorrow, scanning through his pictures yelling, "WHY? WHY? WHY ME, GOD?" But nothing. Quietness struck me internally. I believe it was a combination of the frenzy of men around giving me attention along with my subsiding lust for him.

I wasn't sure how to deal with this new state of mind because I had never been to this place I like to call, "Normal Land." I was afraid to get used to it because I hadn't resided there often, and my time in this delightful place was usually short-lived. I moved on and began to throw my interests to whoever was the cutest or hottest — real mature, I know.

A college woman who is in exploration mode just has to do what she feels and go for it. I kissed so many boys that I should have bought stock in Chapstick. There was a plethora of lips, and there was no harm in checking out the goods. No sex — just first base in all its tongue-turning, slobbery glory. My sorority sisters even provided me with a lovely certificate bestowing me with the title "Suck Face Queen" — twice! I was bursting with pride. And, as one of my friends said, "At least she's not sleeping with them." This was so true, because the thought of a baby or herpes was enough to keep these legs shut tighter than a mafia hit man ratting out his boss. Never gonna happen — and I was too lazy to think about contraceptives.

The College Balancing Act—I'm an Adult, Kind Of

There was so much going on: classes, deciding on a major, work, sorority obligations, and personal life. The process was difficult to master. I was growing into a young adult but still struggling with my inner self, even though I was getting some positive attention from men. I still hadn't completely let go of my physical and mental insecurities, which manifested when I sincerely liked someone. I'd start to get attached, get all nervous, and start squirming around like Charlie Sheen on coke. Calm. Down. Not. Attractive.

I can think back on several potential relationships with first-rate guys who liked me, but they didn't have a shot because I got hooked on a guy a few years into college and could not release my mental grip on him. Luckily, I am not a psycho, and I didn't show this outwardly, but my friends knew. Tom was a charmer and towered over me. His enormous, electric blue eyes and chestnut, curly hair melted me faster than a pina colada in the Caribbean. He exuded confidence. It seeped out of his pores, and that was a giant turn on for me. Chemistry is a funny thing. It gets a hold of you, and you can't shake it, no matter what you do. Our relationship lasted only a few months, but his essence grabbed hold of me like a rabid dog that would not, under *any* circumstances, let go. We had some intense, emotional moments as he confided in me about his sister's death. We held each other all night. He once dropped me off from a date and told me, "You're the pot of gold at the end of the rainbow." I had never heard such a comment. It may have sounded cheesy, but when it came out of his mouth, I swooned. I wonder where he got those lines — maybe from Men Are From Mars, Women Are From Gullible.

Tom grew on me — quickly. He appeared so aloof, yet his mild mannerisms, winks at just the right time, and occasional compliments with his giant, wide smile, took me straight down to helplessness. I needed to be hospitalized, given intense therapy and shock treatments like in the 1940s to knock me out of whatever the hell this was. Tom took over my being like I was hypnotized and Harry Houdini escaped with my mind into another realm. I was so wooed that I could not think straight. It began to be obvious that I was insecure and would fall to pieces when I was deeply in lust. That was *not alluring*, and that is not what men want. I knew this logically but could not apply it. I don't know exactly what I was doing wrong, but I think my vibe changed. When he first liked me, my confidence was really high, and I showed the best of me. As I began to get attached to him, I felt like a switch went off in my head. I began to feel unworthy. Again, the vibe. It's not like I was calling him incessantly or clinging to him. I just withdrew into myself. I have no idea how he actually perceived me, but I could feel it wasn't good. My journey went downhill from there, and he stopped calling. I was left with only obsessive memories and piles of Tom and Lori photos.

After we broke up, I used the mature ploys all smart, sophisticated college women should use (Insert sarcasm). Kissing his friends didn't help; acting like you're having a blast around him didn't work; even inviting him to an event with you after you broke up was no good. I think that's called "desperation."

I could not move on. My mind so wanted to, but my heart was filled with yearning for a relationship that I thought had ended too soon. And that's how I spent the next two years of my college career — pining over a relationship that was never to be.

Two Different Tracks

Thinking back on it, this relationship was pivotal for me. There were two sets of tracks: One was the easy route, where I could let life unfold and relax on the ride; the other was the challenging, rocky course, where self-love was unheard of, and I had to sit in the front seat with bumps and bruises. I followed one set wondering now why I didn't take the other. It's been said, and I do believe, there is no wrong direction. I know we get to where we need to be eventually, yet it still frustrates me to think I wasted so much time. Maybe I could have spared myself so much fretting and emotional pain. It's funny how that just doesn't matter though, does it? I learned many of my life lessons the hard way; I think most of us do.

There is a saying, a book, and a movie called *He's Just Not That Into You.* That was a life-changing notion for me. I agonized for years about the *Why.* Why is he gone? What did I do? High school and college friends wanted to get me through the tortuous moments, but most did not have the guts to tell me why *he was just not into me,* even if they did know. And I wasn't ready to hear what they had to say anyway. But once I got it, my life changed forever.

There could be a number of reasons the relationship ended, but the bottom line is that it wasn't a forever match. I'm not saying that being introspective about a relationship is bad, but when you obsess over the break up to the point of missing other promising opportunities, you're doomed for a while. You miss the chance of finding and falling in love with someone else. The good news is, and you have to believe this, there will be another when you're ready. Your ill fate doesn't have to last forever — unless you allow it to.

The Agony of Dancing on the Party Train

I continued my unconscious spin through an assortment of men. Our Greek system hosted several dances during the year. Sounds like fun, right? Here was the twist: the women had to invite the men. I felt like I was walking the plank into shark-infested waters. I ended up meeting athletes and fraternity men and asking them to these shindigs. I was told a few of them wanted to go out with me; however, through confusion, speculation, and gossip, with a touch of low self-regard and obsessing over the other guy, I ended up with none of them. Are you surprised? I'm not. I'd mess it up by either liking the wrong one or not giving the better choice a chance. I created barriers like Oprah gave away cars. She gave away a car to every single person on one of her shows. She started yelling and pointing to each person saying, "And you get a car, and you get a car, and you get a car." I gave away excuses the same way: "And you are too short, and you aren't cute enough, and you aren't a football player." You name it; I had an excuse for it.

I went to a dance with Dan, a basketball player. He was fun loving, mellow, and attentive, but I didn't get all riled up over him because rumors were circulating that he had a girlfriend. I didn't believe it because what guy would do that? So naïve, Lori. It was also awkward because a rumor was going around that his good friend, another basketball player, liked me. I didn't take him to the dance because I discovered this information too late. Dan and I hung out after the dance, went out a few more times, and of course, there were the usual make-out sessions. A few months later, his coach hosted a local, weekly live TV talk show, and who made an appearance? Dan — with his fiancé! Are you kidding me? And that, my friends, was another good reason for me not to sleep around. That saved me a lot of hurt.

The Uncatchable Fish

But then there was the one that got away. Isn't there

always that *one* who could have been your match? For me, that guy was Bob. He had an appealing, quick wit, and I remember him looking so distinguished at a party in his white, draping toga and his large, green and gold leaf crown. He threw out his arms and danced in circles to "Turning Japanese" by the Vapors like a band of wild cheetahs were chasing him. He was so much fun to watch as he flashed that perfectly white smile and blinked those immense, walnut-colored brown eyes at me while running his hands through his dark chocolate, wavy hair.

He had a high school sweetheart but felt it was time to end it. She was snotty and not his type. He seemed like the kind of guy who would like a more down-to-earth, friendly girl. He was too pleasant and positive for her. He liked me a lot and made that clear. When he saw me in Arby's, our student union of sorts, he would show up right there next to me. I would catch him staring at me with that look that says, "Hey, you're gonna be my woman."

Bob and I used to meet for late afternoon lunches every Friday at this popular little pub around school that served the best thick slices of wheat pizza and beer. We'd sit and talk about anything and everything, but most importantly, he made me laugh. We chatted about the crazy antics that went on at his fraternity house, like the time when he and his brother drove to the grocery store in reverse because the drive shift didn't work. At least they got home safely. Or when his car didn't go above 30 miles per hour, and the police were following him with their sirens on for going too slow — "slow speed chase," he called it. As we talked, he kept his distance but was still flirtatious. He had that look of desire in his eyes, and my gut intuition picked up on it.

Bob did everything right. He met my family for goodness sake! He came to my parents' house, and my mom made lasagna for him and my friends. Our friendship was solid. He had it all, yet I still couldn't let him in. I just couldn't allow myself to be truly loved yet. A few months later, we went on a university ski trip with a bunch of fellow students, and of course, I made out with another guy on the bus — right in front of him. Classy, right? But I had to keep him away. I still couldn't handle the fact that a really great guy wanted me, so I messed it up. I was afraid deep down that I wasn't good enough for him. It didn't help that my ex, Tom from a few years back, was still in my heart. He ended up marrying and divorcing his high school love and having a highly successful career. For many years, I wondered where he was and how he was doing. Could I get that second chance? Or was it not to be? Do you ever wonder where lost loves go? Have they disappeared into the abyss never to be seen or heard from again? Of course not; they're on Facebook.

The number of old friends whose paths cross again on social media is astounding. I did look for Bob and a few others, but by the time I found them, it was too late. They were *taken*. However, sometimes your second chance eventually ends up coming in an unexpected way. We can't dictate the hows and whens of anything. All we can do is stay open so it can find us and not slip through our fingers again. The lesson for me was to keep my eyes, ears, and spidy senses alert — just in case.

The Lasting Lesson I Now Know

I never had more access to men than I did in college, but it didn't matter if one or one hundred guys were available because I was emotionally closed off. I screwed up what could have turned into a lifelong commitment with one of these men I blew off. However, regret can lead to a circle of sorrow, and as American pianist Oscar Levant says, "It's not what you are, it's what you don't become that hurts."

CHAPTER 5

Chugging Along to the Next Stations

The Girl Becomes a Woman—Finally

After college, I hurried into my first professional job, racing to get out of my parents' Dairy Queen and into an official career. I felt this was expected of me because, you know, that's what's *supposed* to happen. My first job was a store manager-in-training for Sherwin-Williams. This was *not* my ultimate job, but I took it anyway to prove to the world that I was moving forward with my life. That's where I met Kaleb. He and I went to training together along with a few others in Cleveland, Ohio. We spent several weeks learning the business by day at one store and learning about each other by night at the bar. It was a perfect breeding ground for partying. We were new college graduates beaming with pride and way too much time and energy on our hands.

I made a conscious decision to see what the fuss was all about, this sex thing. Kaleb and I joked all the time with each other, made fun of our trainer, and just generally goofed around for several weeks. He was not traditionally attractive, with his small frame; thin, larger nose; and beady, dark eyes. But he was as cocky and smart as could be, with confidence oozing out of his eyeballs. I gravitated toward him because unconsciously, I'm sure, I hoped that confidence would rub off on me. One night, we went out for a few cocktails, came back to my room and — had sex! It was so uneventful. I was in shock that it happened without developing any strong feelings for this guy. I was confused because I thought I would latch on when sex was involved, yet I felt very little, if anything, for him. The earth definitely did not move.

A few weeks later after training ended, we went on to our respective stores as managers, and that was it. His store location was about three hours away from mine. He called often for about a year, and I appreciated hearing from him, but it wasn't like I wanted to pack my bags and move to West Virginia. We conversed about our jobs, what we were up to, and even flirted a little. We talked about meeting up, but nothing ever came of it. This experience proved to me that sex alone didn't force me to feel an emotional connection that was just not there. All those years, I built sex up in my head, and I wanted it to be so jubilant. It just wasn't. Sex was meh, and so was this new job. So where would my life and career take me to next?

Stepping Forward and Moving Back Again

Yes, I returned to college — and for another two years. I finally figured out what I wanted to do with my career, and I needed a masters degree to make it happen, so I was off to Youngstown State — again. I was back where all the men were! What a stroke of luck! I was still in my early 20s and at least a bit more mature. Surely, I thought I'd find a great guy this time.

Year one was the Year of Dave, a wonderful man I met through a sorority sister. He didn't attend college, but he was a sweet guy, employed (thank God), and as delectable as a man could be. His demeanor was masculine, yet his personality was light-hearted, ready-for-anything, and airy. He had a perfectly cut, short mullet — business in the front, party in the back (Don't judge me; it was all the rage back then.) — which made him sexy, along with his steel blue eyes. We dated for several months and fell in love. At least I thought my feelings were *in love*. I was attached to Dave but didn't feel that tight instead of solid connection. I only know this now. Back then it just seemed secure, and I desperately wanted that feeling. He did such considerate things for me, like washing my car inside and out while I was working, and he took me on romantic dates. Once, he packed a picturesque picnic lunch of tasty cheeses; an impressive variety of crackers; mouth-watering strawberries; and Miller Lite, the *champagne* of beers, and he fed me as we tailgated before a Pittsburgh Pirates baseball game. The Pirates were his favorite team, not mine, but I didn't let that get in the way of our dreamy date.

Dave came from a kind, giving family who loved me. And I loved them. They accepted me and included me in their daily lives. I often came over after my classes and had dinner with them. Holidays were full of family fun, and they included me in their extremely personal conversations. His mother would get upset when his dad would work on his antique car in the garage because she wanted him to be around her. I thought how lovely that was. After being married for 25 years, she still wanted her husband right by her side. I used to make holiday shirts with one of his sisters, and we spent hours talking about her husband, their child, and her goals in life. Dave's other sister, Katie, was in tenth grade. She and I contemplated boys and how the heck to get through high school with all of its challenges. I thought, "Is he the one?"

At this point, I was allowing myself to love, but my barriers still stood strong. I didn't like that Dave wasn't degreed. He worked in the service department at a car dealership and hoped to take over his dad's position as manager when he retired. I thought that everyone needed a college degree for job security. In my career field of higher education, I probably couldn't stay in my hometown where there weren't even any positions available at the one and only university in the area. All Dave wanted was to buy a home near his parents in town and live happily ever after. I wanted to get away and explore other cities and other career experiences. I certainly wasn't ready to put the apron on, bake apple pies, and pop out any kids.

We didn't tap into each other sexually either, but I tried to overlook it. It was like shoving a square peg into a round hole — pun intended — like two Yangs and no Yin. You know that confused feeling you get when you're bewildered and don't understand what's going on? That was the essence of sex for us. We just didn't unite in the intimacy department. And he was only the second man I had been with in bed.

One day he sat down with me and held my hand, just like all nice guys do when they're about to drop the bomb. He said he knew our relationship wasn't going to last, even though he loved me. He cried, and I cried. Deep down, sex still scared me a bit because of the possibility of getting pregnant. We used condoms, but I wasn't comfortable with myself and didn't know how to verbalize it. I wondered if we were not a fit because of me, him, or both of us. This would plague me for more years to come — more than I'd like to admit. If I had been comfortable with sex, would it have worked out with Dave? Honestly, I don't know.

I did know this was another growth experience, but I still had such a long way to go. I became more aware of my insecurities but allowing only some of them to surface and be dealt with. I learned throughout my life that if I kept shoving my problems under the rug, the floor was eventually going to give way, and everything would come spilling out. Dave ended up marrying one of my sorority sisters; she was my polar opposite in every way — quiet, short, petite, unassuming, and sugar sweet. My hometown is small but not tiny, so this was a strange coincidence, but I don't believe in coincidences. They are incredibly nice people, and I wish them the very best.

It feels cleansing to wish the good ones happiness. It enhances the soul and has allowed me to forgive myself for past mistakes too. The good ones deserve it; they treated me well, and our relationships just didn't work out. I wasn't ready yet to be truly loved anyway. This line of thinking helps me clear the cobwebs of past pain and get going in the right direction again.

Year two of graduate school was the Year of John. I took a major step back in the romance department because I dated someone who was too young for me — almost five years younger. We worked at the same office at the university. We helped first-year students become accustomed to college life with their classes, assisted with campus resources and whatever else they needed to help their experience become the best at YSU. We were able to look to each other for students' answers and guide each other in areas where we had the most collegiate expertise. I was the only grad student, so I had an edge, but John was in the thick of his campus life and knew everything that was happening. We hit it off immediately.

John was a charmer, yet rebellious-looking in a non-threatening way. He looked like a WWE wrestler with his crazy Mohawk with a tail running down his back. His angelic face topped his stocky, masculine body, and his ethereal green eyes sucked me in. It was like aliens came down from the sky and put a spell on me. We went to see Sam Kinison at a small theater in Youngstown. Sam's show was horrible (Maybe he was high on drugs.), but the date with John was remarkable. We spent lots of time just chilling at our families' homes talking about music and school. I often played chauffeur because he shared a car with another family member. We both lived at home, so we never had any privacy. Check out this oddity. At his house, there were only temporary or makeshift doors for the bedrooms and bathroom. They either didn't touch the ceiling, or they were made of beads. I felt like I just stepped into a 1960s LSD party — without the drugs, of course. All of us were just a little too close for comfort. Couples need space and a place to build intimacy.

John taught me that *handsome* isn't everything and that I needed to explore my reasons for taking a step backward. I asked myself, "Are you just looking to fill up the time? Are you fulfilling some fantasy? Are you trying to relive your youth better this time?" I understand now that *charisma* will only take a relationship so far. There has to be more depth and substance, or it will fizzle out like a 2-liter diet coke with a half-open cap sitting in the refrigerator for a month. I believe my mother said it best about my pseudo Hulk Hogan: "He's a nice boy, but he's not the one for you." Enough said.

The Real Grad School Lessons

These graduate school relationships with two completely different types of men taught me something: I was still exploring. I was still seeking out what I liked and needed in men, even though I thought I should have been ready for a more serious commitment. I always want the end result *immediately*! I'm an impatient person, and I continuously learn that lessons often need to be learned prior to taking a next step. I like crossing the finish line before I run the race, but life will have none of that. Whatever I'm pushing through in life needs and will take its own sweet time. As The Beatles so aptly say, "Let It Be."

Another chapter of life ends: successful completion of graduate school, more failed relationships, and time to move on. But where would the train take me next?

CHAPTER 6

Ugh, I Keep Missing the Marriage Stop

I'm Not Really a Loser, Am I?

I was 30 years old, and I thought everything was okay until I was the dateless Maid of Honor in my long-time friend Jessica's wedding. I went through all the repeated motions since I had been in 13 weddings. Yes, lucky 13.

Going to weddings is oh, so much fun. Going in a group feels like high school, but you can't miss the damn thing, or the bride won't ever speak to you again. So you take the dreaded walk of shame into the grand hall of wedding reception glory and proceed straight to the bar. The drinking often helped — a lot. Then you stare at all the couples in whatever type of relationship they are in and wonder, "Are they genuinely happy?" You gulp down some appetizers and wind your way to your dreaded assigned table. What will it be this time? The *Singles* Table? The *Old Maid Aunts* Table? Or even worse, The *Kids* Table? This time, at least I was seated at the head table as I managed to choke down the predictable chicken, rigatoni, and green beans almondine. Usually, I can get through a wedding when I see the cookie and cake tables. Sweets light me up like Jim Carrey on speed, and there's nothing wrong with drowning myself in sugar and vodka tonics too, right?

But this time, I started to cry. I got totally scared and freaked out because I felt *very* alone. Jessica and I were the same age, and I felt like I was lagging behind in the love department. I was surprised this hit me so hard, since it was inevitable that she would get married because of all her mature relationship experience. But I guess this was about me, not her.

After dinner, I decided to sashay in my floor length, deep pink gown over to my parents' table and allow them the pleasure of experiencing my depressive moment. My mom said to my dad, "Talk to your daughter; she's upset about not having a guy." This embarrassed me even further, even though she was stating the obvious. I couldn't believe I was crying at this wedding, and I certainly wasn't crying for joy. It signaled the end of youth for me, and I felt that I was being left out. No engagement party, no wedding, no bridal experience for me. And I had no one on the horizon.

My parents didn't push me about dating. My mom mentioned once, "Not getting married isn't the worst thing that could ever happen to you." She threw out little comments about relationships that didn't portray them in the most positive light. She'd say things like, "You've got life by the ass kid; go have fun. You don't need a man. Don't worry about having kids. If you do, you do; and if not, oh well." She supported my independence, yet when I did seem to have a good thing going with a guy, she was happy for me. She threw me for a loop once, because after a breakup, she asked me if she or Dad had done anything to cause my love life woes. That hit hard because she had never said anything like that to me before. I told her no because I wasn't ready to think about it. In truth, my parents weren't the best relationship role models, but I certainly wasn't going to tell her that. They were wonderful parents who just didn't communicate with each other very well. As life moved on, she never said anything like that again. I think your parents or whoever knows you well not only sees the best in you but also understands your hang ups and flaws. The smartest ones know you'll work them out in your own time and in your own way. I believe my parents knew that. They both had go-with-the-flow personalities. Mine was more intense and energetic, even hyper back then. You know how generations can skip traits. (Thanks, Grandma Dolak.)

Missing the marriage train in your 30s can be quite devastating. No matter where you live, most people believe that you're still young enough, but you better hurry. Traditional society tells you that you can still have kids, and thank God, you still look decent enough for a man to take a second look at you. You're on the brink, so you better move fast, or it's over folks. You'll disappoint your family, yourself, and your God. You're looking down the barrel at 40. What will you do? So what if the worst does happen. What do you *do*?

Keep Stroking That Ego

When your love life sucks, you can always (and probably do) concentrate on other endeavors. Oh, you'll be excellent at something, and you'll probably overdo it because what you lack in one area of your life, you'll make up for in another. You'll need to hang on to something, whether it's your career, your travel adventures, your beauty, your sleek body, or your hobby that you should make a business out of — whatever. Something's gotta get you through this ever-penetrating, mind-numbing experience because it's in the back — or front — of your mind at all times.

So I dove into my career and took my ego with me. I proceeded forward with my masters in counseling with an emphasis in higher education because I felt working with college students was my calling. And being back in the college environment in my comfort zone and getting paid for it seemed like a dream job. I could concentrate on work and all my fine accomplishments and forget about my tragic love life.

Delving into other activities and adventures can be positive. My career kept my ego strong because I was afraid if it didn't, I might fall into a vat of depression. So I took my accolades and degrees and moved out of town. I got my first job working in student services at a college four hours from home. So you'd think that I would have had access to lots of male faculty and businessmen. Nope, I was in Lima, Ohio at a small community college in what I perceived as a small, washed-up industrial town. At least, it was a career starter for me, and I was grateful.

A New Career and New Men

There I met Rick. He was a faculty member in health sciences, the most prestigious area of the college (if there was such a thing). I didn't care for him at first because I was spending my time in another dead end situation. Let's just make a long story short and say that I was developing feelings for a long-time friend who ended up being gay. I knew deep down that he was, but we were steadfast friends — so much so that my head wanted to make it work, even though neither of our hearts could make it happen.

About a year later, I finally took an interest in Rick. He gave me a hard time about making him wait, and I sensed he held grudges just by picking up on his general nasty attitude. His eyes threw daggers at me like they were saying, "You picked the gay dude over me; I was second choice, and I don't know if I can be with someone who made me wait a year." Some major triggers went off in my head immediately, but as usual, I pushed forward, rarely paying attention to my intuition.

Our relationship started out as they usually did. Rick's all into me and I'm riding high like The Real Housewives of Wherever on pain meds. He's calling two to three times a day, making plans with me to go to movies and dinner, still gushing over me even though he was still kind of PO'd at me. Since there wasn't much to do in Lima, we just hung out a lot and talked, listened to music, and partook of the nookie.

He was *not* my type, but he had that *thing* that bowls me over: you've heard it before — confidence. He was short and almost bald, and his face reminded me of Steve Perry from Journey. He was self-deprecating, a smart ass, and a flirt — all at the same time. He teased me a lot, and because I grew up being teased by my dad, it was quite endearing.

One day I was on the phone with a good friend, and he was making fun of us because we had stayed in our hometown for college at The Youngstown State University, the "mighty war" Penguins. I added the adjectives. Penguins aren't that scary or warlike, as you know. He gave us a lot of grief for not branching out and going to college elsewhere, but I guess he didn't notice that I had moved four hours away from home for my current job. He did everything to get on my case. When Youngstown State won it's 2nd National Football Championship, I cut every victory picture out of the *Youngstown Vindicator* and sent it over to his office, just to see what he would do. He proceeded to draw with a black magic marker on each and every picture and write snide comments on them, such as, "Glad to see you defeated the Georgia School for The Blind" and sent them back to me. Have you ever laughed and been pissed at the same time?

He even ended up moving into the apartment right above me. He liked that area of town, and I stupidly let him know that unit was available. This is a horrible idea if you even remotely think you could break up. Can you say, "Awkward"? It was nice being able to just see each other by running up and down a flight of stairs; however, he worked all the time. When he wasn't teaching, he was writing a book or doing anything he could to enhance his career. I felt like second fiddle. When he liked me in the beginning, my confidence was alive and well, like Miss America walking down the runway after winning the crown. As I sincerely began to like him and didn't receive the attention I wanted, my insecurities fled into my consciousness and took over my entire being. That was not attractive to him, as it isn't to most men. So I spent the next year or two with him having all the power. Our relationship was reduced to the occasional hookup, and his feelings for me vanished.

It's no wonder my insecurities raged. I was in the midst of a career crisis, bringing on maniacal stress. College administrators changed the Student Services structure. This meant everything from personnel hirings, firings, new processes, and procedures, and I was in the thick of it all. I was the only one retained working with six new people and a new student philosophy with no training for me or the staff. Working 80 hours a week in a pool of muck meant that I could have used any personal support I could get. It would have been best to just let go, but I clung on to Rick just for some minimal physical affection for several months. About six months later, I got another job. As I was getting ready to leave and stared into my empty apartment for the very last time, I listened to his bed thumping up and down above me and voices moaning with pleasure as he was having sex with another woman. Lesson: Leave when it's over. Period.

Let's sum this up: Boy lusts over girl; girl can do no wrong. Girl is flying high with her newfound power. Girl really starts to like guy and begins to freak out, feels scared, and withdraws from her true wonderful self. Boy gets bored and moves on. Imagine this going on time after time. This was the bane of my relationship existence, and if I didn't figure this out, how would I ever move forward?

Then, the unimaginable happened. It was so life-altering that it changed all of me, every ounce of me — forever.

CHAPTER 7

The Unthinkable Happens: A Tragic Derailment

Could It Get Worse Than This? Nope!

My mom died. She was 58; I was 34. And just like that, the way I looked at the world changed forever. She had been my angel who always put me first. Even though she was strong-willed, she held a soft spot for those she cared about, especially me. I was the love of her life, and even Dad took a back seat. We looked alike, and she laughed at all my crazy antics. She also put up with all my mood swings when I was a kid and had the good sense to know when to back off.

Mom had high blood pressure and clogged arteries, and she could not quit smoking, which apparently also contributed to multiple TIAs, which resulted in lip and eye drooping. When my mom was sick, she planned a trip to Arizona to visit her best friend, my "Aunt" Lucy. Lucy and I planned a secret intervention. Back in the late 90s, you could still get a relative's records straight from the hospital. And that's what I did. I called the facility where she had previously had carotid artery surgery, told them I needed her health records for another doctor, and they agreed. I felt so strange walking through the sanitary, white hallways. I kept thinking, "Am I going to be able to help her? Will she be pissed that I did this? Will she get better?" I snuck her records into her luggage, and she flew west. Poor mom was thinking she was going for rest and relaxation. That was not to be.

After a few days, Aunt Lucy and I dropped the bomb. I told her over the phone, "You're checking into one of the best cardiac hospitals with a world-renowned doctor." She screamed at me so hard, I was taken aback. I'd never heard that kind of tone in her voice — ever! So there she was, stuck with my aunt and me in her ear as my dad sat by passively letting us take the reins. I decided it was best to fly in before surgery. I just could not stay home while this was happening.

While the doctors were clearing another artery, she had a stroke on the table. They gave her medicine, which stopped it momentarily, but as the days went by, she kept having strokes. There were multiple meds, a confusing diagnosis, and more surgery, and then — I got the call from her medical staff. Dad flew in so we could meet at the request of her four doctors. Mom continued to remain unconscious, and they said she would probably never wake up again. Her arms and legs were turning blue. No one knew why. I remember seeing it happen, and I couldn't even verbalize my concerns. I was in shock, and the next day, the blue coloring that looked like frostbite was spreading like tundra taking over a land mass. That land mass was a human being: my mom.

Two weeks had passed since she had flown in for her so-called wonderful trip. I often wonder if she knew that would be the last time she'd ever step foot in her Dairy Queen, that would be the last trip to Arizona, that would be the last time she would see Aunt Lucy, that would be the last time she would feel the warm, dry heat and sun. There were two choices: Keep her hooked up to the machines and amputate the lifeless sections of each of her arms and legs, or let her go. Two weeks after Mom landed in Phoenix, I got back on a plane with my dad. She was on the plane behind us — underneath in cargo.

The Train Derailed and Came to a Screeching Halt, Stopping Just Short of Torpedoing off a Cliff

How could I go on without my mom? Oddly enough, my grandfather passed six weeks later, and my favorite uncle passed six weeks after that. Having a degree in counseling did help a bit, but not that much. I cried the hardest while my mom was in the hospital, but once she died, I became somber. I took charge, as usual. I had to make sure for the first time that my dad was taken care of. I stayed at home with him and commuted 1.5 hours to work each way. I made dinner several nights a week, cleaned, and sat there each night, quietly trying to process what the hell had just happened. There was no cushion on which I could fall anymore. Trying to deal with all this was impossible, so I didn't. I just went about my business living life, like nothing was happening. It took me two full years to grieve, ever so slowly. A few times when I was driving, I cried hysterically. I wondered, "Why cry so hard in the car?" A friend of mine had a theory because it happened to her too when both of her parents passed. She said that being in the car and releasing emotion is safe because you can't lose full control. You still have to drive the darn car. That made sense to me because somewhere in my being, I knew I had to process this slowly to keep my sanity.

Moment of Revelation

When your entire world gets rocked, you have an opportunity to shift your thinking, to look at things in new ways, but more importantly, to begin to understand that not every damn thing is a big deal. Dating and marriage were last on my mind. Once the worst happens to you, your perspective changes, and believe it or not, you can live life more peacefully and even begin to open your heart even wider. Do yourself a favor and embrace the hard lessons coming at you. You'll be so much better for it as life moves on.

Spending time with Dad was good for both of us.

Concurrently, an old flame arose. John from my grad school years showed up at my mom's funeral out of nowhere. We dated a few months, and he disappeared. You'd think I would have been distraught, but I make this comment to this day about many issues in life: *Nothing, and I mean nothing, could happen to me that's worse than what's already happened.* Life is put into perspective when the closest person to you is gone.

John got me through an extremely hard time, which was his purpose of coming back. I remember my mom saying so many years ago, "He's a nice guy, but he's not the one for you." And as usual, she was right. But I thank you, John, for being there when I needed you most.

CHAPTER 8

All Aboard! Moving Along Again in the Right Direction

New Beginnings

As I inched my way forward from Mom's death, my perception of the world changed. I looked at people differently, and life situations were a bit easier to manage. Nothing was a big deal. I shifted my perspective and changed my priorities. Something must have been marinating deep inside of me because a total reroute was on its way.

I reconnected with some friends I had worked with in the past. Rosie was a passionate, hot-tempered, beautiful, voluptuous Latina, and she brought me into her world of friends and family. I had never experienced anything like that because my family sheltered me from anyone who didn't look like me. My new friends opened up my world to new experiences and love. I met Tommy at a party. I fell in lust so hard, my head whirled. I had to have him at almost any cost. I had not felt this way in — well, never! Even my old flame Tom didn't compare to Tommy. He was as extroverted as they come, a hot-blooded Puerto Rican man around my age. He was short, husky, ridiculously handsome, and loads of fun. He had these giant, dark doe-like eyes with lizard-like thick eyelids and olive skin. His laugh was like fireworks going off, and he laughed all day long. He was always *on* and lived every moment of life to its fullest.

He was kind of single, as another woman floated in and out of his life. He was endearing and passionate about anything that was in front of him. I'd get him a ham and cheese Panini sandwich with an egg on it, and he'd drool over it like he'd just won the million-dollar, scratch-off ticket that he'd bought at the gas station that morning.

Oddly, he loved my crazy personality. He cracked up at everything I said, and that motivated me to keep being myself. I felt light-hearted, free and fun as opposed to closed-off and withdrawn around men I really adored. Once I experienced this and realized I had never been my real self, I knew I could never go back. I knew I had been trapped in a tunnel, unable to breathe with the walls caving in on me. Finally, after what felt like forever, I saw a light in my path. I ran at lightening speed toward it because if I stayed in that tunnel, I knew I'd eventually die. I was going to break free and be me, no matter what. It was an awakening!

I spent the next five years in a tumultuous relationship with Tommy. Complicating matters, he lived in another city six hours away. And he had not completely released that other woman from his life, so we were on and off for our first few years. I was angry, but I pressed on because, well, I loved him and more importantly, I wanted the validation he gave me. I adored being around him no matter what because he made me feel a way I never had before. I loved the joy of saying whatever I wanted when I wanted to. For the most part, my filter was on hold, as I spewed my dumb, often irreverent jokes and acted like a kid on the highest roller coaster on the planet. We took the short, one-hour flight back and forth to each other's homes and spent long weekends playing and loving together. We toured our respective cities, went to movies, or simply laughed and talked. I felt free around him — and freedom is a human's most precious need. You don't give that up easily. I would always remember this lesson and never let it go.

The last three years in our relationship, we moved along and even discussed marriage. I knew that would be a disaster, especially when Tommy informed me that he believed that oral sex was not cheating. *Really?* That's like saying a yeast infection is one of life's pure joys — puh-leeze. I had hoped to the heavens he was kidding, but I knew he wasn't. I figured he was exploring other activities with other women, but I made a conscious decision not to think about it if I couldn't prove it.

Fun was fun, but eventually, his antics were going to catch up with us. After all this time, I knew his M.O., but I was going to ride this out as long as I needed to. One day we were talking on the phone, and he mentioned something about his life issues and needing some counseling, and that was it. We hung up, never to speak again — after five years! Crazy as it seems, I was not that surprised. He was an all or nothing guy, and I made it tough to argue with me. What was there to fight about? But, as I suspected, there was more to it.

The Right Direction Detour

I began to shut down mentally. I wasn't conscious of what was happening to me yet. I couldn't sleep at night, and the only comfortable position I could get into was turning myself completely around and sleeping at the foot of the bed. I got out of bed at the very last minute in order to get to work on time.

There was a slow, painful ache inside me all day, every day, especially at work. I'd get through it by meeting up for lunch with close friends who took my mind off of this slow, tortuous burn. People know me as totally focused and driven, and that was not happening. Part of my job was to create and plan programs for employers as well as put together continuing education classes for the public. I had a difficult time just trying to get an email out. Much gratitude for my assistant, who kept things afloat while I resided in my funk.

Believe it or not, no one around me at work said anything. I think my presence at the time was so off-putting and unusual that people just didn't know how to react to me. I was aloof and reclusive in my office. I talked to no one unless I was forced, and coworkers seemed to back away when it came time to ask me to do anything extra or out of the ordinary.

Maybe I scared people with this dramatic change in myself. I am so grateful I was left alone to get through it because I don't know how I would have reacted to any extra pushing from anyone.

I spent free time in solitude unless I was with neighbors on the weekends. I drowned myself in alcohol to hide from the needling agony that was shot into me and spread poison through my heart. This situation was not a down moment; this was full throttle depression. I had been talking to my friend Ron about this, and he begged me over several weeks to get to the doctor. I refused to go. I didn't want any medication because I am sensitive to them. If I take two Ibuprofen, I pass out into a deep slumber and don't wake up for eight hours. I just wanted to get through it on my own, and frankly, I was at such a low point, I didn't even care about making an appointment.

One day I was driving home from work down a quiet,

state route. The area is fairly sparse, populated with only a few houses and small farms in massive spaces filled with grass and trees. A large semi was passing me on the other side of the small, two-lane road, and I slowly closed my eyes but kept my hands on the wheel. I could hear the sound of the truck getting closer, and I said to myself, "If the truck hits you, it's okay."

After it passed, I opened my eyes and kept driving. I knew at that moment that I was beginning to give up. I wasn't completely sure I wanted to die; ambivalence took over. I just wanted to talk to my mother and be done on Earth. I didn't see anything promising for me on the horizon.

The truck incident occurred two more times before I told Ron what had happened. He went into full crazy mode on me, sent over his doctor's number, and told me if I didn't call within a day, he would do it for me. I knew he meant it, so I picked up the phone and reluctantly made the call.

Dr. Joan Thomas turned out to be the best doctor I ever had. She asked me what had brought me in that day, and I lost it. Tears came rolling down as Hurricane Lori was whirling at a Level 5. I was so embarrassed, and she soothed my soul by explaining that I had to let out my feelings to someone who could help me. And that she did. For the next two years, I was on a very light dose of anxiety medication that changed my life.

Revving Up the Engine Again

This was so bizarre. I popped straight back into myself in less than a week! That low tolerance for meds paid off because I could handle whatever was coming my way. I was back on the rails. My career success resumed, and I felt like myself again — focused, more lively, and most importantly, able to function in the world again.

A mutual friend made Tommy call me about six months later, and he left a voicemail — something about his "being in town, hopes I'm well, blah, blah, blah" — but it was obviously over. I gained what I needed from this relationship and never cried. I can't believe I didn't cry. I was borderline suicidal, but darn it, I never cried. A year went by, and I learned from a mutual friend that he had gotten one woman pregnant, then met another half his age, and married her six weeks after meeting her. This should have surprised me, but it didn't. I was finally allowing myself to let go and move on. I didn't have the wherewithal to see that I only needed him in my life to learn lessons, good and bad.

A Breakthrough Revelation

Mom's death and all the life lessons that were coming along with it enabled me to gain strength. My internal growth from Mom's passing and my former lovers were teaching me that being my real self was key to finding an astonishing male partner. No matter how hard I tried, and I did try, nothing was going to make anyone do anything their heart wasn't having. I could not change a man. I could only change myself and control my reactions, no one else's. I needed to relax and let go a little bit.

After all, I was going to be turning forty soon. I thought I'd take a little time off, recoup from the Tommy madness, and regroup later. What I didn't know was that later would be *much* later.

But now? It was time to upgrade my ticket on the journey of happiness, and that's exactly what happened.

CHAPTER 9

Stopping at the Depot for a Breather

Alone in the Full Swing of Life

When I turned forty, I decided to throw myself a Hawaiian Luau party. I was thin and looking good — pretty. Yes, I finally said it! The *thin* part was probably as a result of the Tommy breakup. I always lost weight after a split, since my diet was the only thing I could control, and taking off a few pounds made me feel better. About fifty people were jammed inside and outside of my 1100 square-foot condo — all with their multi-colored festive Hawaiian leis, flowered shirts, beige grass skirts and giant, juiced-up cocktails. Even Ariel, the little dog that lived across the street came, wearing her little hula skirt and lei with the orange, red, blue, and yellow flowers.

As the 1990s music channel blared from my TV and the

kitchen blender whirred with dark Puerto Rican rum, ice, and tasty strawberries and bananas, my life-long friend Kris made an unforgettable comment. She said, "You know what, Cuz? (That's what we called each other.) The 40s are going to be *your* decade." For some reason, her words totally resonated with me. I believed her. She didn't know much about my old boyfriends because we didn't see each other all the time, but I think she just had a gut sense. So did I. I allowed that comment to say with me for the entire decade.

Hibernating to Heal

It was clearly time for a break. I always took a hiatus between men, sometimes for a year or even two. I needed time to lick my wounds and soothe my ego. I'd read some self-help book either about relationships or becoming a *better me*. Yes, I always learned something, but my pattern of relationship grieving was pretty much the same every time. Wallow, wallow, withdraw, wallow some more, and then move on. Sounds fun, right?

Somehow, this break turned into something else. I spent four — yes, I said *four* — years dateless. I took time alone to a new level. Without having any conscious knowledge of it, I moved forward with everyday life as if I would be alone forever. I spent my days working overtime, and I used my weeknights to exercise, watch movies, or try one of my new moneymaking schemes like flipping houses. I spent every possible moment doing anything but thinking about men and relationships.

And weekends — they were the best. I had an exceptional group of people living right on my street. Many of them were single or had spouses, but I spent much of my time with two single guys. Our platonic union meant fun all the time with no drama. We watched sporting events at my house, went out to sports bars, and attended sporting events. We even took mini vacations together to a playful little island in Ohio on Lake Erie filled with bars, beaches, and music called Put-In-Bay. We went to concerts, hosted neighborhood parties, and celebrated many holidays together. There's never a dull moment when you fill your time with friends, right?

As many of my other buddies moved away, the three of us still held tight. I created my social life around them, and I didn't have to think about anything except our next escapade. If I needed a date for a wedding, I could ask one of them — or both! I could bring them along to family events if they wanted something to do. And what about those infamous romantic times of the year like Valentine's Day? We could care less as long as we laughed our way through it.

Now you may be wondering, "Lori, didn't you like either of these guys, or didn't they have girlfriends?" Fair question. Luckily for me, they were confirmed bachelors, and we all had been in the friend zone so long, the idea of hooking up seemed preposterous. After a while though, I started to fall into distress. My outlet was cocktails — too many of them. I could not sleep through a night, and I woke up listless and melancholy. The sauce was pouring through me and out into a vat of sadness. It's so easy to take the path of least resistance when there's always someone next door ready and willing to hobnob or team up with a glass or bottle in hand. This lifestyle finally began to wear a little bit thin.

My Surprise Seatmate

Then she, yes she, came along — the love of my life!

Remember my neighbor's dog, Ariel, who came to my 40th Birthday Hawaiian Luau? Over the past few years, she had found her way to my condo; that is, she escaped out her front door if she saw me anywhere around. I was falling in *like*. She was so unique: half Bichon and half Hairless Chinese Crested. She had the best features of both breeds — all white hair with one dark gray ear. She weighed only 12 pounds, had a long, hairy tail and giant, coffee-colored eyes. The ends of her sky-high ears seeped into her water bowl, and as she drank, she looked like she could take off into the sky like *The Flying Nun*. (OK, I'm dating myself. It's an old sitcom from the 70s.)

We took such a liking to each other that the current owners asked me to watch her when they went on vacation. I never had a pet in my life, except a fish that I forgot to feed when I was seven. I realized that Ariel needed some medical attention because she was scratching her ears incessantly. They stunk too, so I knew something had to be seriously wrong with this adorable pup. I ended up taking care of her and spending hundreds of dollars at the vet. I didn't care as long as she felt well. She ended up having a double ear infection that was so bad, it took a year and a half before it finally cleared up for good! She also had a urinary tract infection, and we weren't sure if she was ever caught up on her shots.

My neighbors were so grateful I took care of her, but I had to tell a little white lie. I didn't want them to know I was paying for all of Ariel's care because I knew they would be upset with me. I danced around the subject, saying I had a friend who was a vet, and she took care of it. I brought her back to them good as new. At the time, they were dealing with their young daughter's health issues, so I decided to help out. Plus, Ariel was having an effect on me I wasn't used to. I was having motherly instincts that screamed, "Take care of this dog-child now!" I didn't understand at the time what the heck was going on with me.

As time went on, she occasionally stayed overnight. My neighbors' youngest child continued to need extra attention, so the time and care they could spend on Ariel became limited. They got incredibly angry with her behavior problems like burrowing through their screen door, digging into the trash, or ripping into poopy diapers. I ended up coming to the rescue. I cleaned Ariel, give her kisses and treats, and cuddled with her for hours. I even bought her an expensive cage because they kept her in a travel cage several hours a day, which made me crazy. She could hardly move! They allowed me to let her out each day, and by the next year, I took care of her for another week when they went on vacation.

Something totally unexpected happened when I went to give her back. I burst into tears — and not any old salty drops. I'm talking hysterics, so much so that the man of the family teared up. I apologized over and over, telling them that I guessed I had gotten too attached. You see, I had never needed to take care of anything before. These feelings were foreign to me, and I did not understand what was happening.

The good news for both Ariel and me was that the lady of the house was *over* this sweet canine. Her husband was on the fence, but the kicker was their eldest daughter, who was eight years old at the time. Hannah said to her mom, "Mommy, that's Lori's dog, not ours." Many of my neighbors often sensed that she was an old soul by the way she acted and reacted to life. She was mature beyond her years and knew something we didn't. That little sweetie was willing to give up her dog in our best interest, and it was definitely the best thing for both Ariel *and* me.

Ariel changed my life. When I first met her, she had the physical ailments, and I had the spiritual ones. We both needed some help. I didn't know what was missing in my life. After all, you can't miss what you never had. Being an only child with no children of my own, and at the time, no spouse, I could just focus on myself and not pay that much attention to my surroundings. I came and went as I pleased while trying to be a decent person who had a little fun along the way. I found myself distraught when she was sick and almost inconsolable when she had cancer. And I remember when she got clipped by that 10-speed bike racing past us. But the little twelve-pound warrior came out of all those challenges shining with that special glow in those big, brown, beautiful eyes. I, on the other hand, was trudging through life. She cuddled with me when I cried and made me laugh every day with her crazy antics and ballsy attitude. She needed me — and boy, did I need her. For the first time, I had the responsibility of taking care of a living creature that had more needs than a goldfish.

Caring for Ariel deepened me emotionally, opening up much more love than I knew I had within me. I rarely ever said "I love you" to anyone, and I said it several times a day to her. As time passed, that love began to transfer to other people, which allowed my heart to open and expand exponentially to the point that I had grown into a more expansive version of myself.

Teachers Can Sometimes Have Four Legs

Yes, I have multiple degrees from a reputable university, but Ariel taught me life lessons.

If someone, animal *or* human, comes into your life, and you know with every ounce of your being that you need to be in each other's lives, do it. Even if it's not easy and the lessons are hard but so worthwhile, do it. Some souls will push you hard out of your comfort zone. But when you come out on the other side, you are changed for good. That is growth, and that can never be taken from you. That growth will benefit you in all your endeavors for the rest of your life.

Starting to Come Alive Again

I loved learning what it meant to be a *dog mom,* but

something was tugging at me, pulling me from the inside out. The urge was back, and it was time to break out from my cocoon and get back into the dating world again. With the help of Mom's death cracking my heart open and Ariel's existence giving me life, I began to burst alive like a volcano erupting in the Himalayas. I was healing, and my mental and physical being was ready for whatever came my way.

So then came Eric. We met at speed dating. I thought I'd try something different, so what the heck? I was running late for the event and was so nervous, I almost wet my pants. I just made it on time. The event was in a private room at a classy bar. The small seats and square tables were positioned in a circular fashion with twelve men moving around to meet each of the twelve women. I saw Eric way before he got to me. I knew right away there was no one else in this group I was attracted to except him.

I dated lots of men throughout the years with various looks from pasty white to Italian to Latino, but I wasn't sure what Eric's race even was. He could have been Mulatto, Latino, Middle Eastern, Native American, or some combination of all of that. He was the variety pack with lots of flavors all mixed in. He was bald with a goatee and luscious lips. I tended to gravitate to this type of look, and on top of all that, he was tall, smart, and well traveled. Yum.

We only got a precious few minutes to talk to each guy before they yelled, "Time to move on!" But in our allotted time, we discussed our mutual love of sports, what we did for a living, where we called home — all the usual small talk stuff. We even took a minute to chat about our passions. We learned that we both loved to travel and enjoyed the Cleveland scene immensely with its eclectic music, museums, Playhouse Square, and the tantalizing, ethnic and contemporary food choices.

My gut is usually right on, as we seemed to connect. Some people went to the bar afterward, but we didn't. We talked a bit after and then went our separate ways. I anxiously waited to hear from him first. Would we just be friends, business acquaintances, or date bait? The only way to know if either of us wanted to take it to the next level was to check the speed dating website. I decided not to do anything for twenty-four hours. I was trying to stay calm and demure, which is never easy for me when I'm initially attracted to someone.

The next day, I was at the airport waiting to leave for

a business trip and checked my inbox from the website. I saw he had sent me a message, and my heart raced like Richard Petty speeding into the finish line at the Indy 500. I was getting a little dizzy too! There were three options on the site to choose from: date, friends, and business. He picked "date!" As fearful as I was, I was back in the game. I clicked "date" as well; however, he didn't call for a few days, so I wrote him a very quick email stating that I was glad we had met and looked forward to seeing him soon. Was it confident or a little desperate? I wasn't sure, but six hours later, which seemed like a lifetime, he said he was sorry he had taken so long to respond, but he had been in meetings all day. We planned our first date a week later.

As all my previous suitors did, Eric won me over like Fred Astaire swooping Ginger Rogers right off her feet. He called all the time, did what he said he would do, and graced me lavishly with attention. We spent time downtown at restaurants and a jazz club called Club 59, with its oversized martinis and hip vibe. He got us tickets to the Rock and Roll Hall of Fame ceremony the year Metallica was inducted, and we jammed for hours to all types of music.

I got a new bed, and Eric drove thirty miles that day

just to set it up for me so I would not have to figure it out (mechanically inclined I'm not). We all remember what lust is like. We put on our best show for the other, and we want to believe that this is how the person really is. Our hearts pound with anticipation of the next text or phone call. When he picks us up for a date, our heart flutters a little, and when he kisses us, we swoon, or our stomach starts bouncing around like we're going to puke.

He knew some of my story, including my four-year break, and he kept reminding me that I now had a boyfriend and I should get used to this wonderful new way of life. I desperately wanted to buy into what he was saying.

On a five-day vacation to Fort Myers, Florida, we lay on the beach all day long with our rum fruit punches — he chilling out to his jams, and I listening to the ocean and enjoying the salty, airy breeze. He called it our *starter vacation,* meaning if we could make it through this, we would go somewhere farther away for a longer period of time. I thought to myself, "Huh, what kinds of issues does he think we are going to have on vacation?" At night, we sat on our patio and talked or ventured out to check out the little town, holding hands as couples in love do. A few days in, he blew up at me for no reason. I remember his telling me he always got into one major argument with a woman when they went on vacation. That's weird, and frankly, unnecessary. Vacation seemed like a sucky time to fight. He got mad because I was in the shower too long, yet I said I wanted to get going to dinner quickly. He had said he was in no hurry, so why all of a sudden was it a monumental problem that I was taking so long in the shower? His behavior just did not make sense to me, and it totally angered me. It's not that easy to fight with me. I do not like drama, so I guess he had to make up something to get in that one vacation fight. After a sleepless night, he made up with me, but from that point on, I began to feel just a tad uneasy about him. There was that gut instinct again trying to creep in.

We dated a little under a year. Overall, we were a strong couple, but something was holding us back. I loved Eric, and at the same time, I felt a sense of uneasiness about our relationship. I told him once that we resonated as a couple at about 85%. He disagreed and said, "No, 100% for sure." I knew that I was not totally being myself. I was subconsciously figuring out that ultimately, we were not a match. However, I was too enthralled with him to fully accept this and let him go. I wanted to keep trying. Instead, he made the decision for us.

My free-spirited boyfriend decided it was time to explore other opportunities. He said, " I just can't do this anymore." Translation? He couldn't be with *me* anymore. I didn't know what happened. Nothing really did happen — no major, blow out fight. I guess he just grew apart from *us.* That 85% was never going to become 100%. But I had changed. I was more open, a more loving person. How could this happen — again? I was pissed!

So I did what I normally would *not* do. I started dating right away. There was no way I was going back into my shell again.

I tried online dating and meet-up groups. For the first time in my life, still hurting, I went on dates and joined in on activities, looking for men who had the same interests as I. I did what Dr. Phil says: "Ya gotta get out there where the men are." There was no stopping me. I was a whirlwind of energy making dating my number one priority.

I dated a slew of men a few times, even a few months, but none of them interested me. I dated Josh, and John, and Todd, and Mike — whoever. Eric was still on my mind. Every once in a while, he texted me, and I perceived him to be, well, open to me again. Then we finally met one on one, and the feelings rushed back to me so intensely I felt nauseous. We continued to talk on the phone several times over several months, hung out occasionally, and kissed sometimes. My instincts told me this wasn't going to work, even though he kept me hanging on, and I gladly took any little piece of him he would give me.

I always had to figure out what I did wrong. The blame I put on myself this time was that the sex wasn't as spontaneous as it should be, so I needed to fix it. This older woman still had her youthful panic of getting pregnant, and at this point, I was in the No Kids Allowed zone. I made my mind up years ago that raising children was not in my wheelhouse. I tried many birth control methods, and none of them was a *fit* for me. Hormone adjustments turned me into the Wicked Witch of Northeast Ohio who ate ice cream for breakfast and spewed rudeness to anyone who walked her path. Joan Crawford and her wire hangers had nothing on me! Finally, after years of searching, I found something that I didn't know existed!

I had never explored a non hormonal IUD, and it was the perfect fit. So now I was off to the races — full steam ahead — free of this issue and able to love fully.

A Moment of Clarity

Interestingly, when it was time to try out my new solution, I realized something: I did not trust Eric. I knew it in my soul, and my inner self tugged at me whispering, "Move on… Move on." He was finished with us long ago when we broke up, but I couldn't accept it. Truth be told, I don't believe anything would have made us the right couple. Not even the best orgasm in the world can fix what isn't there. I should have listened to the real me inside and loved myself enough to know that I could and would get to that 100%. I thought at the time that 85% was good enough. It wasn't, and it never will be!

Thank you, Eric, for bringing me back to life and back to love again. I am forever grateful.

CHAPTER 10

Onward Again: The Glimmer at the End of the Tunnel

Practicing What I Preach

It was time to start paying attention to what I knew was right. No more excuses! I finally knew the real deal: if a man wants you, he will do everything in his power to make it happen. I saw this occur with other couples, but I could not apply it to myself. Well, that line of thinking was over. I was at my wit's end!

I made a radical decision: **no man would ever break up with me again!** Strong, gutsy words coming from a woman who was probably just intensely mad again, right? No way, friends; this was for real. I sat with one of my closest friends and told her my profound commitment.

If anyone would be a skeptic and put me in my place, she would. She was my no B.S. friend who challenged me and even played devil's advocate when I needed it. Her reaction to my comment was, "I believe you." Without question, I was ready to show the world the true me.

Others always envied my life because I could do whatever I wanted when I wanted. Most of my choices only affected me and maybe Ariel. I had an incredible group of friends, went on trips to clear blue waters, and threw dozens of blowout parties like around-the-world feasts and sporting extravaganzas, but it didn't matter because my love life was substandard and unacceptable to me.

In the past, I had no gratitude for my life experiences, allowing what brought me down to always blind me from what was happening. My buried head in the sand kept me from appreciating the joy and learning I was experiencing. I missed out on so much, and it was going to stop — right then!

Taking Myself to the Next Level—The Epiphany

As this realization sank in fully, I continued to gain

this sense of assurance, confidence at the highest level, which had never happened to me before. I felt positive, peaceful, and happy. I floated along in this place for about six months. Then one day, I was walking the love of my life, Ariel, down a road right near my home. I still remember the exact spot. My street was coming up on my left in about twenty feet, and we were near a little stream of water with a guardrail on the right. I stopped dead in my tracks . . . and a thought struck me like a lightening bolt jolted right through my body.

"My life is perfect!" came into my consciousness as an all-consuming wave of knowledge that permeated my body from my head down to my toes. I felt awakened and completely clear headed. Previously, I had felt left out of loving partnerships, like I was in a glass-enclosed case wanting to be recognized and loved. Men could *see* me, but they couldn't *get through* to me. Everything *looked* normal to the outsider, yet it wasn't. The opening was always right there to break free and walk through, but I could not do it. I was trapped by my fears, but at that moment, I finally had the courage to open the damn door! I just walked out into freedom and light. And all was easier. *Finally!*

I stood silently and looked around. Then, a subtle, divine-like lightness came over me, and I felt surprisingly comfortable with life. I was touched by an overarching aura of peace, and my self-imposed shackles just unlocked with ease as I walked away from all the previous pain. The neighborhood looked the same, the trees were still in their upright positions, cars were still moving along, and people were still walking, yet everything was new and different. My perspective of the world around me completely shifted. I don't remember the rest of the walk that day. I guess I was in a bit of shock.

Moment of Reflection

As my radically changed self, I walked out of the door every day feeling altered and ethereal. With head held high, I looked at men, and people in general, differently. I started to notice opportunities for friendship and love that I didn't see before. I saw men more for who they actually were. Chemistry still mattered, but I was attracted to more men with more substantial qualities like ethics, commitment, and mental strength. I was now allowing myself to see more of the real *them* because I now knew who the *real me* was — confident, mentally strong, and now able to love fully. *Sexy* meant something different, like kindness, genuineness, and maturity. The ability for a man to open his heart fully and see the beauty in me inside and out was happening because I was allowing it to for the first time! I began to open a mental space and invite more people to interact with me on my interpersonal playground. It felt so good to believe in myself and be able to offer a partner a complete, full-fledged version of myself. I now could love with every inch of my soul, and I knew no one would ever take that from me again.

Living Life to the Fullest

What did I do next? The answer was . . . drum roll, please, "Who cares?" Yes, who cares? I needed to forget it all and just live, for goodness sake. That's what came naturally, so I did it. I began to appreciate life and all it had to offer. When I was outside, I noticed my surroundings and the beauty of nature, like the sun beaming down or a pensive bird sitting on my fence. I became much more tolerant of people and even complimented them.

If someone annoyed me, I let go of it so much easier and became more flexible and creative with any problems that arose on my schedule. Most everything could be adjusted or was fixable. If someone was late on a call, there was no use getting upset. Change it or move on. Life's too short.

I took notice when positive things happened, and I was thankful. If I received some delightful surprise or found extra money, I was grateful. One year, I inherited over four thousand dollars that I didn't know about from my mom's life insurance policy. I wanted a new piece of exercise equipment and wasn't sure if I wanted to dole out two grand. One day, my neighbor walked out into his driveway and said to me, "Hey, I have this bicycle type thing, and I want to get rid of it since I'm moving." I asked, "How much?" He told me it was free, and he even put it in my house. It's no surprise that these things began to happen much more frequently after I opened my mind.

Most importantly, I chilled the heck out. I knew everything was not a big deal. I used to be jealous of others, especially those in seemingly fantastic relationships; I now admired them and was pleased to know happy couples existed. I had good feelings when I spent time with them. If my friends were meeting and connecting with the partner of their dreams, I was sincerely happy for them. In the past, a piece of me wanted them to be miserable right beside me. Not anymore.

Let me be clear. I did not care if I met anyone or stayed without a partner for the rest of my life. I knew my experience was incredible, just as it was.

I wished everyone well, and it was easy because life wasn't just about me and my sorrows anymore. I focused on excitement and happiness. I flitted through life with a smile, taking in every lesson and working through every challenge with much more ease. After all those turbulent years, I owed it to myself to try coasting along.

CHAPTER 11

Finally—The Love Train Arrives at the Depot

A Relationship in the Making

Have you ever heard of women who try everything from unique intercourse techniques to fertility drugs and everything in between and they still can't get pregnant? Then, after years of emotional and physical trauma to their bodies, minds, and spirits, they finally adopt a child. Less than a year later, they magically get pregnant and deliver a perfectly healthy baby. How is this possible? Research on this is still mixed, and there is no exact answer.

It's the same with relationships. You try, but you mess up over and over again. You finally get frustrated enough and decide to let it all go. You give up for a while and just go it alone. You have some kicks, forget about finding the perfect partner, and all of a sudden, he shows up — right in front of your eyes.

Meeting my future husband and love of my life, Ryan, was not love at first sight for me. I think it was for him, though. Don't get me wrong; he was adorable — all 6'2" of him and his soon-to-be-bald head, with a smile that makes a girl feel giddy. And what could be better? He's a former college basketball player. I'm guessing I'm still somewhat enticed by jocks, because let's face it, they have fit bodies, and they're suave and self-assured. Sorry — some leftover business from high school and college days still lies within me. I was not sold at first because I thought he was kind of quirky. I have attracted quirky before but never quirky *and* fascinating. He had this air about him that seemed so gentle and kind, yet manly and self-reliant at the same time. I had to remember that I'm pretty odd at times too. Like attracts like, and distinctive attracts distinctive apparently.

Sometimes Ryan made awkward gestures with his hands when he was reacting to something that made him get all riled up. He threw his arms up in the air, and at first, I thought, "Where are we, the zoo?" He also clapped with intense vigor when people made comments that excited him, and he repeated his infamous sayings like, "Let's get buckled in." This meant, "Watch this football game with all the intensity you can muster." "Too much sidebar" meant, "Stop talking so much; I'm trying to watch the game." But then he would open his mouth and with that deep, manly voice say something so bizarre or sexual that it made me laugh or get frisky.

I didn't know what to make of this guy. I had never met anyone like him.

My friend Melissa decided to tell him some stories about our outings to the Lake Erie Islands when we were in our twenties. We often partied with the single men who docked their boats there, and after a few too many cocktails, I may have made out with a few of these men. Well, he has *never* let me forget it, so much so that he calls me "Lovie Boat" or just "Boat" every day — and I mean *every day.* He does not let things go and will drive something into the ground until there is not a parcel left of it. Over time, I learned to embrace my nickname and be proud of it, so much so that I jokingly suggested if we ever got married, he should engrave it on his wedding band.

I met Ryan through our mutual good friend, Chris. He and his wife, Dawn, were my neighbors for sixteen years, and Chris was Ryan's best friend growing up. Ryan isn't much of a drinker, but Chris invited him to a local neighborhood sports bar to watch basketball one weekend evening. Ryan had moved back to town after a sorrowful divorce to help his mother take care of his dad who was struck with cancer. I almost ran past them looking for other friends until Chris saw me out of the corner of his eye and jumped right out in front of me. "Bah!" he screamed, as he hurled out in front of me! The three of us talked for the next several hours, and they decided to stop at my place after the game. Ryan looked around with a strange look on his face. I cocked my head and said, "What?" He asked if he was on *Candid Camera* because he noticed I had a few pieces of Dallas Cowboys paraphernalia around my condo. He has loved the Cowboys since he was a kid, and so have I. I found out later that he dreamed of being with a partner who enjoyed sports as much as he. I asked him if he wanted to see my Roger Staubach navy jersey, and he looked at me like he had just seen a ghost. I came downstairs wearing it, and he has not left my side since.

Dawn is known for being the voice of reason, and I talked with her several times while Ryan and I were dating. I'd tell her some story about him and his unusual personality, and she always laughed like crazy and said, "That's our Betta (Ryan's life-long nickname); I love him. He's the best guy ever. Give him a shot." After talking with her more, I finally began to *get* him.

We discussed sports way too much, even for my liking, yet I could see his loving nature. He's a one-woman man, has the ethics of Pope Francis, and was raised by an extraordinary family that showed support, love, and kindness.

He told me stories about his family. Ryan's dad wore a toupee, and he laid it on a mannequin head every night. This thing scared the hell out of his younger cousins at their many family gatherings and became the source of jokes for years. And Ryan adores his son. I learned about his Friday night playtime with his son in their basement where they built mini train sets and played until they both passed out on the floor. We shared stories about our college days, Greek life, and our mutual love for all kinds of music. He interned at 98.5, a major Cleveland rock station, and I absorbed every story about the stars he met like John

Fogerty, Vince Neil, and local celeb Michael Stanley.

Then a bomb dropped that could send a couple spinning. Seven months into our dating history, Ryan's dad passed away in September 2013, and after all the services and life celebrations were over, he needed to get away by himself. But twenty minutes out of town, he got this shocking call from me: "Ryan, I don't know how to tell you this. My dad just died." Yes, our fathers died five days apart. He turned his car right around and went through another painful funeral all over again. To make matters worse, we both had to make significant job changes that year because of organizational restructuring. This led to some time off from work for both of us until we found acceptable work situations. Ryan stood by me through thick and thin and has not, even for one minute, ever wavered in his love for me. I have done the same for him. Ryan was sweet, kind, dependable, and supportive.

Love Is Here, and I'm Ready

I finally understand what my mother always tried to tell me: "He's got to love you just a little more than you love him." This may not be a popular comment, but it rings true for me. I watched people experience this; I understood the words, but I could not grasp the concept until Ryan came into my life. Being with him was *so easy.* He called when he said he would, picked me up on time, and showed his affection easily. He didn't lie, play hard to get, or make excuses. He treated me like a goddess, fulfilling my every need. After several months of dating, he continued to create special moments for me. As he opened the car door for me, there was my favorite drink, a fresh iced tea. Then, he would turn on one of my favorite Led Zeppelin songs ("Thank You") and lay a Dallas Cowboys blanket on my lap (favorite team) to make sure I'd stay warm on a cool evening.

He just naturally became the best boyfriend *ever.*

Early on in our relationship, I spent several weekends with neighbors watching sports, and I just wanted to stay around my house. One night, I neglected to check in with him when I promised I would, and after he called me several times without my answering, he got very upset with me. The next morning, he didn't want to speak to me or see me. I felt horrible, so I took a peace offering of milk and doughnuts over to his house. He told me he wanted to take the day away from each other. I handed all the goodies over and took off. Over the next few hours, he called back, and we talked it all out calmly. It was one of those opportunities that allowed us to come to a mutual understanding about each other's needs. Better yet, we agreed on how to handle our communication and specific life situations so they would not likely happen again. Bonus — win-win. These situations gave us the chance to grow our relationship. The old Lori would have been too insecure for that. She would have freaked out about the tiff and prepared herself for the break up with a box of tissues, a good book, and a call to her best buddy Melissa for some heartfelt reassurance that it wasn't her fault.

Moment of Clarity

We all need to acknowledge and appreciate our own growth. I have broken the pattern of my parent's poor communication skills and moved on to healthy discussions in my loving partnership with Ryan. Whether our talks are around finances, (That's a hard one.) serious life issues like living arrangements and career change, or just reveling in life's good times, we talk it out. We have the best serious talks walking Ariel and the best light-hearted talks while lying in bed before sleep. I don't recommend discussing serious issues right before bed. I did that once, and Ryan was up half the night with worry.

I had to be tolerant and patient. So not me. I liked to be free and do what I wanted because, well, I was used to it. Luckily, I found a man who accepts and supports my independence. I still make time for my friends, and when I need alone time, he understands. I enjoy my wine tours and parties, and I'm okay if he doesn't like to do those things with me all the time. I still have to make sure I'm playing fair with him. I have to think of him, his life, and his needs. I had to fit him into my life, and he had to do the same for me. I also had to make room for his almost teenage son, and "Stepmommy Dearest" (which is what I've asked Nicholas to call me, and he won't) had to go from a duo to a trio every other weekend, which I've never experienced before. This also means that my home gets messier, and I have to be more accountable. I don't get to just take off and head out of town on a whim without discussing it. Being in a mature relationship requires adjustments, flexibility, a lot of thank yous, and even some I'm sorrys.

I don't like the word *sacrifice,* but I think it's the best word to describe what we do in relationships. It's tough for me to look at it that way because I'm more of an abundance thinker; there's always enough of what one needs, no taking away. So I try to spin the sacrifice in a way that doesn't feel like I'm giving anything up but doing something different or new. Perhaps I might even like the change it brings. A good attitude helps immensely. Ryan's son likes to play the Wii, and I never loved playing games until I gave in and kicked some butt in Wii bowling. I got so involved that I threw my arm into the air with such thrust, I broke a glass candle into a plethora of tiny pieces when I was making my potential strike.

Sometimes being aware and making sure that I'm paying attention to Ryan can be a struggle. When I get focused, I'm like a bear spotting its next meal at your cabin in the woods — not moving my eyes away from the prize for a second. Must. Get. The. Food. Imagine how exciting it is for Ryan when I can't take my eyes off the computer, and he's trying to talk with me or kiss me. It's tough, but I have to stop, breathe, and remember that there is another human being in my life. He deserves some of me too.

Acceptance is major. Sometimes Ryan reminds me to accept him as he is. Then I say, um . . . *no*. Kidding aside, this is tough for many people, but I stay focused on the good because he has so much of it. For example, every night after work, he sits with me, gives me a leg and foot massage, and pays attention to what I say and need. That alone is worth its weight in gold. I'm still challenged in the acceptance arena, but I make an effort every day because I'm pretty idiosyncratic too.

I've let him in, checked him out, and at times, even tested him and our relationship. My autonomy as a woman in her early 50s is a strong force in my life. I'm a *do-what-I-want-to-do-when-I-want-to-do-it* person, but Ryan's laid-back nature allows him to understand my need to flourish and strive, even if at times he just needs to go along with me for the ride. If I must work, write, or prepare for a presentation, he realizes that I need the space to do that without making me feel guilty. At the same time, I have had to realize when I should be there for him, not as the end-of-the-day, exhausted me, but as the wide awake, energetic me.

I had gotten on and off the love train for decades while dragging around my heavy, self-doubt. It was time to abandon that heavy baggage and travel lightly. I was in my 40s when I not only learned — but absolutely grasped — what it would take to be open minded enough to allow an ideal partner into my life. I met Ryan when I was 48 years old.

Let's Celebrate!

So often we forget to celebrate what we've been waiting for our entire lives. I overcame getting in my own way. I allowed myself to love me — Me, with all my flaws and challenges — Me, who is unique and an admirable person — Me, who now has compassion, love, and light to offer back to the world. Congratulations to Me. You did it, girl!

I love Ryan, and as of this writing, we are engaged. By the time you read this book, I will be married — one day into my 53rd birthday. I will be married — *finally.*

CHAPTER 12

Keeping My Relationship on Track

The Journey Continues

I finally did it. I found love — love of myself and love of another. So now what? Ryan and I agreed that marriage was the next step. How do I even process this word *marriage?* It brings angst to some and pure joy to others. On the one hand, the divorce rate is over 50%; on the other hand, I see a real life picture of a couple in their nineties lying in bed holding each other's hands like they're in their 20s, and my heart melts. I talk to someone going through a bitter divorce, and it scares me. Then I'm reminded of my favorite couples that show each other patience, kindness, and physical affection after 30 years of marriage. What's a woman to think?

There are many variables at play here. The scariest one is the unknown. How in the blazes am I supposed to know who I'm going to be in ten or even five years? Many couples say, "We just grew apart." How is *that* supposed to instill confidence in anyone either looking for or advancing their current relationship? It doesn't.

Just about all personal challenges come down to one thing: *fear.* Whether or not the prevalent feeling is anger, insecurity, anxiety, or even depression, when it comes down to it, fear is the base emotion. Sure, everyone in a relationship pays lip service to how wonderful their life is going to be together; then it's not. So I've decided to take my fear of fear to a new and better place.

I'm going to do my best to be *mindful* on a daily basis about what is going on between my partner and me. Wide-eyed and bushy-tailed, I'm going into this like Goldie Hawn and Kurt Russell. They've been together thirty-four years, and Goldie's advice is, "Sex is very important." She also says, "Stay mindful of who and what we love about each other, always have that aspect of being turned on by that person and sometimes when they really make you mad, you need to sit down and say 'Ya but…' "Kurt's advice is, "At the end of the day, love conquers all and that's all you can go with." Short and sweet, Kurt, but the point is, show conscious love for the other person. Living with my eyes wide open is the catalyst to being attentive to my partner. My hope is that this awareness allows me to catch a problem before it gets out of hand. If one of us is spending too much time doing something else, and we're not planning time to connect each day, then we have to correct that. Ryan likes to say, "No slacking off with us." This means if we are mentally or physically elsewhere, we need to get real and deal with it.

One weekend, I was writing this book, and I was on a roll for many hours into the evening. He gently walked upstairs and shut the door. I just knew that he needed time with me, so I wrote a bit more, put some notes down, turned off the computer, and met him in bed. He said, "I knew you'd show up." He was so happy, and it was so worth it! My partner realizes a couple of things: This writing will not go on forever; I still made some time for us; and it's important I follow my passion. Fortunately, he gets me, because at times I'm so focused I barely remember to go potty. I'm not kidding!

I've observed so many lost partnership connections with

those who have kids. Even though I will have a stepson in my life, it's not the same as living the daily life of a family with children. It's so easy to get caught up in *the kids*. It seems to me that those folks have to make an even stronger effort to set aside some time for themselves *and* their relationship. I'm not saying it's easy; I'm saying it's necessary. Cart them off to the grandparents' or auntie's house. They'll fill them with sugar, let them stay up all night, and the kids will sleep until noon. The couple gets their quiet time together and maybe even a good romp in the sack!

Work and technology can be a considerable interference too, and I'm seriously becoming plagued in these areas. Did you ever think there would come a day when you had to pay thousands of dollars to go somewhere to disconnect from technology? That's called going back to the 1980s, people. There are those of us addicted to our phones, and it's causing real problems in our lives. Are we paying attention to how we communicate with each other as we sit at the dinner table staring at our devices, or are we even having dinner together?

I hope to remember this mantra: Relationships are

everything, *and* my loved ones are the most important of them all.

Managing the Unexpected

We can be aware as ever, yet life happens. Our partner gets physically sick, falls into a mental funk, or both. Perhaps there is a job loss or a move to an undesired city to stay employed. Numerous problems can occur, and then the dreaded word I can't stand comes up: *compromise.* I don't like that word because it often means finding the in-between; then both parties lose. I prefer *negotiation.* You get this, and I get that, and we can still both live comfortably with the outcome. Okay, call it compromising if you want; I'm just not going to call it that.

I want to move to the Caribbean. Ryan does too, and when we think about family, finances, and timing, we realize it won't be today, and perhaps we will just live there a few months of the year. That was not my original intention, but once I thought through the pros and cons, it may be the best fit for us.

Open mindedness is an important human trait. When I take a step back and think through the many options of a situation, I often realize that there is more than one good answer. I believe this will be helpful in my marriage. Some may still call it compromising; I call it a triumph for two!

And if that doesn't work, I'll leave him for a Bahamian surfer — just kidding.

Overcoming Boredom

So we're just sitting around one day starring at each other. Or, more likely, we're staring at our phones. The honeymoon is over, right? The excitement of learning about each other may have worn off a bit. Intimacy is good but maybe a bit repetitive. Is this it? Scary!

I'm not at the boring stage yet, but I know one thing: I better have a couple of tools at my disposal because I'm going to need them. First, I'm never bored. I delight in even simple activities like watching TV or reading. I can't expect to be entertained by my significant other, so I need to enjoy myself and my life. Have you ever heard that saying, "If you're bored, that means you're the one who's boring"? I believe that because boredom is a mindset, and it's up to me to be in that headspace or not.

Having passions is key. I have a few of them like walking,

reading, watching sports, and *The Bachelor,* (which admittedly is my guilty pleasure). I just love when Johnny acts like he doesn't know who he wants three measly days before asking Susie to marry him. So wrong, yet so entertaining. Please don't hate me. Sharing some of my passions with my beloved makes life vibrant. It's not necessary that he participate in all of my activities, but I want Ryan to care about some of them and be genuinely interested in going for the ride alongside me. This creates stimulating conversation, as it bonds us together even more. However, *The Bachelor* is off limits because as he says, "Please don't torture me anymore."

I adore dogs so much so that I find myself connecting with them and their owners. I enjoy coming home and telling the tales of what Fido did today and sharing pictures and stories. Ryan didn't grow up or even think that much about our canine friends, but after he met me, he has become so much more open and affectionate with them.

Ryan loves sports — most all sports — twenty-four-hours-a-day sports. Luckily, I do too, but not as much as he. We watch at home and go to lots of football games and love the experience. However, when I've had enough, I have learned just to do something else. He needs to do his thing to be happy too. Who am I to deny him that?

You Spoiled, Rotten Brat

This is a tender area for me. I am an only child who was given an abundance of material things; however, I was *not* allowed to treat my family and others like a jerk. I was put in my place when necessary. I am lucky that my fiancé is extremely laid back so I can take charge, which is my style. After all the extroverts I dated, the quiet one ended up being the right fit for me. Makes you wonder: how much do we think about personality compatibility when it comes to our match? Opposites attracting, when the characteristics of each other flow well together, can be a beautiful thing. When they continuously cause havoc, however, perhaps it's time to rethink if the relationship is meant for the long term.

Brats often struggle in relationships if everything has to be about them. I *cannot* win all the time, even though I secretly wish I could. But I do find it easy to concede when it doesn't matter at all. If I'm trying to win for the sake of winning, I might be in for some dire times ahead, don't you think? The bottom line is there are so many challenges that can and will arise. It all comes down to my attitude and my willingness to be the best person I can be as often as possible.

Choosing the Light Side

I just don't have the emotional wherewithal to suffer anymore. I'm too tired. Aren't we all? It's just easier to allow the right person into your life, and it's healthier to stop worrying and relax. I am amazed how often people say they are going to *work on it* or *try harder* with their partners, when deep down, the relationship is either going to work or it isn't. I'm not saying a couple shouldn't try, but there's a limit. All this misery and constant, never-ending struggle will eventually suck the life out of all of us. We know when it's over; we can feel it *if* we trust ourselves. It took me 48 years to learn that lesson.

A few years ago, I decided to go with my gut and my heart to allow only men into my life who were *a good fit.* This meant no drama — only emotionally available, moral, kind souls. It took a long time to get there, but once I met one of these fine gentlemen, I went for it, and I got it! After all those years of utter angst, frankly, it just wasn't that hard to find him once I was *open* to him. I wish I'd have known how to accomplish this twenty years ago, but I believe we get to where we need to be when we're ready.

It's a wonder how many times I merged onto the other train track just to be derailed in the end. I was like the roadrunner getting smashed into nothingness, then bouncing right back up only to get run over again. Ouch — that hurts like hell after awhile! Exploring the possibilities while dating and deciding if a relationship will work out or not is simply much easier. Now we know what a monumental task this can be when you find yourself *falling* for him or her. All the lust can blind you as you toil your way through the tunnel of love.

You'll hear couples tell you that they fight like crazy, don't have many of the same values, and annoy each other on a daily basis, and they wouldn't have it any other way. They call it challenging, even fun at times! I think it's too much work, stress, and chaotic over the long haul. I choose kindness, support, and calm. I couldn't enter into marriage without it. I don't think anyone should.

Relationship Advice from the Passenger on the Train

It All Starts with You

Listen, friends. I know you've heard this before, but I *cannot* emphasize this enough. **You *must* like yourself before any relationship can flourish for you.** I know stunning women can get guys even if they are a hot mess, yet I do believe that it does catch up with them eventually.

To know if you're ready for a partner, think about a few things: How do you talk to yourself? Healthy self-talk means giving yourself a break when you screw up. We are all human, and it's okay to let go and forgive. If you constantly berate yourself inside or outside for that matter, stop it. If you say words like, "You're such an idiot.

I can't believe I did that. Nothing ever works out for me," you will not only insist they are true, but this talk will also eat away at your self-confidence, if you even had any in the first place.

Catch yourself the minute you do it, and gently press the "Off" button. Just relax and let it go because it doesn't serve you in any way. No one says this is easy, but it's crucial.

How's your self-esteem? I'll tell you how you know if it's good. Do you laugh at your mistakes? Are you careful not to take criticism too much to heart? Can you let it go if someone makes negative comments about you or your work?

If you're a bit of a jerk, then maybe you have some work to do on yourself. However, if you're a decent human being, then that's all the world can expect from you. You're only human; you're not supposed to be perfect!

If you're obsessing about your looks, your weight, your significant other, or anything else, there is a problem. Understand that if you don't get this straightened out, you will not be able to establish the basis of a good relationship. You need to come to the table with your best mental self to even have a chance to succeed. Remember, as two people progress in a relationship, you both will begin to let your guard down and show your true selves. As your individuality comes forth, your flaws will appear, and the same will happen with your partner. When we give ourselves a break, we typically do the same for other people. This is necessary if a partnership is going to work.

Begin to notice and admire your strengths. Revel in them, and practice doing more of them. You will always have definite qualities that you cannot or will not change. If you can live with that, then stop worrying about them. Accept your uniqueness, knowing that not everyone will be on board with you. Have the sauciness to say, "That's okay. You be you, and I'll be me."

The kicker is you have to feel it deep down to your core. No lip service — only authentic feelings of self love and acceptance. If you need a little help to do this, get it. Every person deserves to feel their finest in order to put their best into the world.

Don't be afraid of your weaknesses like I was. The right person will accept them — maybe even embrace them. You'll need the wherewithal to say, "Who cares? I'm me, and if we are not a match, I wish you well." Have the faith to know that the right person will come to you.

Balance Is the Key to Life

Everywhere I go, I say, "Balance." This word comes up in the counseling classes I teach, when I'm conversing with friends, or doing a presentation. What balance means to you may be different from what it means to me. Overall, I believe you have balance if you feel pretty happy with life. You have to be in tune with your feelings to know. You've probably heard the terms "Mind, Body, Spirit." Do you have adequate time in your life to pay attention to all of those areas? Time seems to be a problem for most people. You can't be emotionally healthy, take care of your body, or grow toward self-actualization without having moments of quiet space to do that.

Ask yourself where you want to be in those areas. The more you have your life within your control, the better prepared you are for an outstanding partner. The more commitment you have to your own growth, the stronger relationship you will have.

You will know when you are out of balance. You get sick,

more annoyed at your life and people in it, turn to habits that aren't good for you, and either get too much sleep or not enough. You aren't getting what you need, and you may or may not even realize it.

It's an uncomfortable feeling, to say the least. You end up in this place for a variety of reasons. If another person is throwing you out of whack, this can get tough. You have to take a long, hard look at what this person brings to your life and make some decisions about their need to be in it. Sometimes this person is a relative, longtime friend, or even a current partner. I'm not saying this is easy, but you must take care of yourself to allow the best to happen to you. Seek some help if you're not sure how to approach the people in your life. You'll end up having challenging discussions with them, or maybe you'll know it's time for you and them to move on. Either way, you must have the belief in yourself that no matter what, you're the most important person, and you need to honor that.

Compassion Shows Strength

What does compassion mean when it comes to loving yourself? It means being less judgmental and kind. Are we able to forgive ourselves? When you are able to do this, you are more than likely to turn the cheek for others. This gift portrays love, and people are attracted to it. The crucial element is if you don't end up forgiving, your resentment will eat you alive!

I am not suggesting that you be a pushover. Respecting yourself is number one. At the same time, when you do forgive, you have two choices. You can forgive and part ways, wishing others well knowing that you learned valuable lessons. Or you can forgive and forget because you have a healthy relationship with that person.

Maybe you make excuses for people. That's an indication to pay attention and work on your own issues. If the excuse is: "I know he won't lie again," yet he's lied several times before, take a hard look at why you're protecting this person. Is it because deep down you're afraid — afraid you'll never get anyone better or anyone else? That's a self esteem problem. Or maybe this person has been around forever and you just don't see your life without this person in it. The question is: Do they still bring you happiness with the utmost respect towards you, or are there more harsh times than good? Only you know, and if you're honest with yourself, the answer is right in front of you. However, being open to hearing it is the key.

Maybe there is something in your youth that needs forgiving. Do what you have to do to allow that to happen. Your past was a long time ago, and you're a different person — all grown up now (at least chronologically). Loving yourself is the only answer because putting the best *you* forward brings light into the world and the right person into your life. The essential element here is you can always have compassion, whether you're kicking a partner out of your life or showing more love toward yourself or another wonderful human being.

Gratitude Is Life Changing

There is nothing easier to incorporate in your life than gratitude. There is much research about what it can do for your well-being and how it can change your life in the most incredible ways. I use it daily. If something is going off the rails, I immediately think about, or better yet, write down everything I can think of at that moment for which I am grateful. My attitude instantly shifts to a much better place. When I'm in that positive space, life takes a turn for the more pleasant, and I go on having a much better day.

There are even times when I'm upset at someone, and I remember all the good things they bring to my life. I use it with wonderful people who may have just aggravated me momentarily. People who hurt me tend to fall out of my world eventually, so there's no need for me to deal with them. I still thank them for the lesson though.

Showing gratitude brings on a mindset shift. If you are looking to get into a relationship, improve a current one, or get over a former love, using this gift will help you have a better life overall. Not only will your day-to-day life improve but your relationships with everyone will also be better. When you are reminded of the good and you focus on it, people pick up on that from your general demeanor. It's not only attractive to partners; it also shows itself to all who are part of your life. Best of all, it makes you feel like a million bucks. Who doesn't want that?

Whenever I was in a quandary about a relationship issue, I created a gratitude list and said it out loud while I was driving. Sometimes it was about the guy; other times it was more broad. Over time, my general openness to the truth allowed me to make the decision that honored me. If a relationship was over, it may not have been easy, but when I looked, no matter how nice he could be, how handsome he was, or how much I loved his many positive qualities, I knew he wasn't able to support my soul. Although I often cried for a long time, letting go of him allowed my beloved to arrive.

What If Your Beloved Isn't Showing Up?

So you're working on yourself. You should be so proud, because there's nothing more important than each human being putting their best self forward. It's good for you and humanity. However, this love connection is taking longer than you'd hoped. *Where is he or she?* I get it. I was 48 years old before I met Ryan. Just keep on living, loving, and appreciating each day. It's all you can and need to do.

We give ourselves a break when we acknowledge that we do things when we are genuinely ready. I realize society has its rules and expectations; however, we are not cookie-cutter human beings. How well can you deal with that? It used to eat me alive, yet over time, I began to ask, "Who gives a crap?" I'm not hurting anyone. I'm on my own path, and I will get there when it's right for me. For some it may mean experiencing life non traditionally, such as adopting children instead of producing biologically or getting married over 50, like me.

If you try to rush it, you end up doing a disservice to yourself because you can't get to where you need to be if you just aren't there yet. Now there's some logic for you, but it's true. I understand this concept may be tough to get your arms around, so patience is a must. Just continue doing what feels right. Look at the opportunities coming to you, and if they feel appropriate, take them. One by one, take them.

I used to get so anxious about, well . . . everything. Now, not so much. I calmed down and realized that everyone around my age was already married and moving forward, and that wasn't my path. I needed to do other things in this world during those times when everyone else was having babies and buying their mini vans. Once I accepted that, everything fell into place.

Don't Ever Give Up

Hope is all we have, and it's essential. Once you truly

believe that you can have what you want, that's most of the battle. So end the conflict within yourself. It's time your internal war was over. Know that your growth makes a better life for yourself. You are feeling your best, and with that good things come. Maybe they come in ways that seem strange or unexpected. Maybe they come in the form of a partner that you had no idea you would fall in love with. Maybe you end up with opportunities that change your life in the most unexpected, thrilling ways. It happened to me. Why wouldn't it happen to you? All you need to do is allow your life to unfold while feeling your best.

My partner was not what I expected. Previously, I didn't allow men who were gentle, loving, and kind into my life. My eyes couldn't see the ones who were rock solid and treated me like the princess I am. By the way, we are all princes and princesses. My former low self worth was not having any of that. In my best Arnold Schwarzenegger voice, I say, "Must have de bad boy who has his own agenda and only looks out for himself." When you love yourself unconditionally, you'll open up to all kinds of new possibilities, and the world will look different. Just watch and admire its evolution.

What Does It Mean to Be Happy?

For goodness sake, just have some fun. We are supposed to take our journey with all the bumps and thrills going on simultaneously. If every experience was always wonderful, there would be no way to know what we wholeheartedly want. Enjoy every moment of the adventure believing that there are always more fabulous times ahead. Because there are.

My most sincere wish for you, kind reader, is that you allow yourself to accept and cherish your time here on this planet and that you let go of what you can't control, knowing that life takes its course. You might as well be happy living it, because frankly, the alternative sucks.

Take lots of long, deep breaths, smile, and laugh a lot. Have an extraordinary time, whether or not your partner is showing up. If you do these things, you'll have a better shot that they *will* appear. But most of all, stay focused on putting love into the universe. In the end, nothing else will matter anyway.

Our time in this world is short. Consider ourselves fortunate that we've been granted a ticket to hop aboard this life's train. Even with all its starts, stops, and continuous winding turns, we surged ahead. We've made it through the dark tunnels that freaked us out and have even been derailed at times. But in the end, there's always another route to explore, allowing us additional opportunities to love, granting time to replenish our souls, and most importantly, providing us another chance to grow into the remarkable person we were always meant to be.

About the Author

Lori A. Peters is a writer who has been featured and published in media outlets, including *Huffington Post*, *Your Tango*, *Brides*, and *Fox News* Magazine. Lori's first book, *Getting Married at Last: My Journey from Hopelessness to Happiness* is available on Amazon in paperback and Kindle.

She also provides numerous professional and entertaining presentations around happiness and well-being for various types of audiences. Her Happiness Hangout® Radio Show on bbsradio has gained thousands of listeners, as she and her guests dive into deep and interesting topics around personal relationship happiness.

Lori is proud of her 25-year career in higher education, having earned her bachelors in business and her masters in counseling and higher education. Currently, she is a college instructor in social sciences. She has also been offering personal development presentations for over 25 years. Lori facilitates Live Happy-Live Better, a customizable program for various audiences who want to enhance their happiness in personal or professional relationships or increase well-being in their lives. She also volunteers on a national level and had the opportunity to be part of a team that runs a major nonprofit with over 100,000 members. She is passionate about work-life balance, relationships, and helping people to feel their best during times of challenge.

Resources

Check out all her resources and information, and sign up for her FREE Happiness Hangout® Quick Reads at www.happinesshangout.net

Lori A. Peters

Email:

happyhangout@gmail.com

Facebook:

www.facebook.com/happinesshangout.net

Twitter:

www.twitter.com/happyhangout

LinkedIn:

www.linkedin.com/pub/lori-peters/6/b91/3b9

Website:

www.HappinessHangout.net

Videos:

www.youtube.com/channel/UC3BDJh9Zzixn3MV7k3-RjKw

Media Outlets

Radio: Happiness Hangout Show:

www.bbsradio.com/happinesshangout

Your Tango — over 13 million unique readers per month:

www.yourtango.com/experts/lori-peters

The Magic Happens Magazine:

www.themagichappensnow.com/author/happy/

Syndicated and Published articles:

Your Tango, Huffington Post, Brides, Fox News,

All for Women, Pop Sugar

The Happiness Hangout®

The Happiness Hangout® is the place to grow and support your loving partnerships through books, articles, videos, presentations, classes, my blog, and my radio show. Participate, gain new and exciting knowledge, and watch how your communication skills will soar to the next level in your relationships. Come hang out as often as you like. This is the place to get what you need to have a happier loving union with your partner.

Happiness Hangout® Presentations
Live Happy-Live Better

Enhance your happiness level during this entertaining and interactive presentation. Everyone wants to feel their best, especially during their most challenging times. We will discuss how to raise and keep your level of happiness higher and the magic formula to feeling your best as your life changes and transitions over time. Our time will be well spent in group participation as well as in interactive exercises that will help you get and keep you in the positive mindset. The program can be focused on personal and professional relationships.

Programs can be done in a short format, keynote, or lengthier workshop. They are effective for personal development days, wellness days, corporate events, and conferences. All programs include lively participant and presenter interactions, exercises, and videos if technology is available.

Contact for pricing options:

happyhangout@gmail.com

Testimonials

- *"Lori is such a professional. She has been a guest speaker for several of my corporate clients, and her presentations are thoroughly enjoyable and incredibly informative. I look forward to have her return."*

  Kim Hemminger, RN, BSN, CHNC, Health and Wellness Manager, Wellness Works for You

- *"Lori Peters is an outstanding presenter. She does a great job engaging her audience with practical and meaningful content. The participants left her program motivated with information they could put to use immediately."*

  Cyndi McCabe, Job Placement Coordinator, Lorain County Community College

- *"Lori has been a presenter for our organization numerous times at our conventions/local chapters. Her speaking style is lively, fun, and energetic. She is always well prepared for the audience and can go off the cuff when needed. I would highly recommend her for personal development topics at conferences or at your next event."*

  Keeley McDonald, Zeta Tau Alpha
  Former National President

- *"Having experienced Lori's presentations in both personal development and volunteer management over the last several years, I would urge anyone looking for a speaker to have Lori at their next event. Lori's dynamic and energizing presentations are done effortlessly and will leave you wanting more. Inviting her to your event should be on your must-do list. You'll be happy you did!"*

  Beth Rush, Children's Librarian and Volunteer

- *"Lori has represented my business in a very dynamic way. She speaks to large groups in an entertaining and informative way, and they respond to her very well. I would highly recommend her to speak at your next event!"*

Michael Krysiak, Owner and President,
Aire Serv of Strongsville

- *"I have been part of the audience when Lori has provided presentations to various networking, educational, and civic groups. I would highly recommend her, as she has an energetic and interactive style that connects with audiences."*

Lena Knight, Midpoint Campus Center Coordinator

- *"I worked directly with Lori in a management, training, and supervising capacity. She frequently trained small and large groups of volunteers in various volunteer management topics and personal development. Lori is organized, efficient and fun, and her speaking style is energetic and inspiring! Consider Lori as your speaker at your next event."*

Helen Fish, Former ZTA National Council

- *"She would be a top-notch presenter for your event in the area of personal development/well-being and happiness."*

Edd Krammer, Owner, Aire Serv of Mentor

Gratitude Journal Information

Lori Peters, Happiness Hangout®

I am so pleased to provide you this gift as a small token of my appreciation for purchasing my book. Positive Psychology research tells us that gratitude is one of the best ways to help us feel happier.

Here are some ways that I hope help you feel your best, especially during times of challenge:

Journaling

I know what you're asking. When am I going to have time to do that? The good news is you can complete this in a very short period of time and reap the benefits immediately.

There Are Many Ways to Do This:

- Each day write down 3-5 good things that happened to you that day. They can be the smallest of things, like someone told you they liked your coat or a stranger gave you 5 cents so you didn't have to break a dollar.

- Write down five things for which you are grateful. Again, they can be very small things.

- Write down a great gratitude situation that you experienced.

Gratitude Journal Ideas
Consider Writing On:

- Things you love to do
- Ways you like to help others
- Everyone you appreciate
- Positive things about people you don't like
- Upcoming fun activities
- Everything good that happened the day before
- All those you love and why
- What's positive about your job
- What's positive about your family

- The best day you've ever had
- Your dream job/dream life/dream mate
- Your passions
- Your best strengths
- Best vacation ever or a future vacation

A Gift to Others Is a Gift to Yourself

These Tips Can Help You Raise Joy in Your Life and Others:

- Make it a point to say something nice to at least one person when you are out of your home. People love it, and you really make their day.

- Take the above and do the same with those you live with.

- You may be pretty good at using social media to be thankful, but if you're not, it's a great addition to your time online.

- Now get off social media and call or write a thank you note to someone. Let them know of a situation or maybe just how much you appreciate them. It shows that you took a little extra time on their behalf.

- When you receive excellent service, write a review online. Reviews are one of the most important things for companies because it increases their business.
- Be extra kind to those who serve you in any way. They are doing their best.
- Try to find the good in a tough situation.

Gratitude Rants

Throughout your day, anytime, but especially when you're stressed, take just a minute to do a Gratitude Rant. In that moment, think of everything for which you are happy—everything. Don't stop until you've got nothing left; then think of a few more.

I often do this when I'm in the car or somewhere where I can't do anything else. Other places to do this activity:

- Waiting for kids at events or school
- Waiting for appointments (Yes, you can put down the phone for a few minutes.)
- While in any mode of transportation, like planes, trains, and automobiles
- During times of solitude
- While taking care of personal hygiene (LOL)

- While doing a menial task like washing the car and cooking dinner

You Feel Better When Your State
of Mind Is in a Better Place

Want more information on gratitude? Go to my site, and sign up for my Happiness Quick Reads:

www.happinesshangout.net

Happiness Hangout® Blogs

For all my latest blogs, check out my website at:

www.happinesshangout.net

Please enjoy one of my articles from my blog.

How Using Gratitude Can Create the Love Life You Crave

Interested in getting the relationship of your dreams or spicing up the one you already have? Give thanks not only to your partner but also to everyone who crosses your path. Now I'm not talking about running up to strangers and thanking them for no reason, but you should praise those who deserve it. Does this sound strange? That's ok. Read on, and find out how life changing it is to use gratitude. First, let's look at just some of the facts from *Forbes.com:*

"Gratitude improves physical health. Grateful people experience fewer aches and pains and they report feeling healthier than other people, according to a 2012 study published in Personality and Individual Differences."

"Gratitude improves psychological health. Robert A. Emmons, Ph.D., a leading gratitude researcher, has conducted multiple studies on the link between gratitude and well-being. His research confirms that gratitude effectively increases happiness and reduces depression."

"Gratitude improves self-esteem. Rather than becoming resentful toward people who have more money or better jobs — which is a major factor in reduced self-esteem — grateful people are able to appreciate other people's accomplishments."

Gratitude Also Can Boost Your Relationship in Wonderful, Meaningful Ways

1. Catch Them Doing Something Right.

We hear this term used a lot with parenting. Why not use it with all your loved ones? Let's say your partner does something out of the norm, like carry the laundry, wash your car, or pick up a morning drink for you. Make a bigger deal about it. Let them know how sweet it was and add a little kiss on top. Your partner loves it and will actually do more of it if they feel that true appreciation.

2. Appreciate the Everyday Mundane Things Happening to You.

Do you have the attitude of expectation? I deserve this and my partner should do this for me. That is a mistake, my friends! Human beings want to know they matter, even when they're doing the most humdrum tasks. Think about what they do for you on a constant basis and take notice. Maybe your partner cleans up the kitchen after dinner each night or takes the trash out every week. Yuck! Aren't you glad you don't have to do it?

Be extra thankful; give them a hug or even better, a tap on the butt for their continuous effort. They will enjoy the extra attention, whether they show it or not.

3. Do Small Things for Your Beloved.

It only takes a minute to do something special. Help your lover out. Pick up a sock or run an errand to make their lives easier. This is especially easy when you are out and about anyway. You could even purchase a mini gift that you know they will love. I picked up a package of Reese Cups one day, and you'd think I gave my man a million bucks.

4. Be Grateful to Your Ex.

I'm not kidding here. I know it's hard, if not nearly impossible, especially if that person seemed cruel and unusual. However, didn't past relationships help you learn valuable lessons about who you are and what you want in a partner? Perhaps you even viewed yourself in a new way knowing that you are too special not to have the person of your dreams.

Thank them in your journal or any gratitude exercise you do. You must release this person and let the anger go so Mr. or Ms. Right can actually show up. Forgiving them doesn't mean they can just come back into your life. It means you're letting go and moving forward without holding on to regret or angst. You can't take that garbage into a potentially meaningful union.

5. Create a Couples or Individual Journal.

Journaling has multiple life benefits. *The Huffington Post* says: "It raises your IQ, helps you achieve your goals and helps release worry and build self-confidence."

Perhaps one of its greatest uses is mindfulness. *The Huffington Post* adds, "It's the buzz word for good reason. There's a strong connection between happiness and mindfulness. Journaling brings you into that state of mindfulness; past frustrations and future anxieties lose their edge in the present moment. It calls a wandering mind to attention, from passivity to actively engaging with your thoughts."

Take pen to paper and write down the good you see in each other each day. Read it to the other person and watch your love life soar. If you're single, write about the good things you did today. It will build your self-esteem, and you need that to allow a great person into your life.

6. Create a Bedtime Gratitude Exercise.

Take a few minutes before bedtime and do some deep breathing exercises to relax. Hold hands and remind each other how much you appreciate them in the good and challenging times. You decide how you want to make it special for both of you. Not only is this a phenomenal bonding experience but it also sends you off to a night of pleasant, sweet dreams.

You can also do this exercise alone. Just take the emphasis from them to you.

It really isn't that tough to be grateful. Being grateful is just about being conscious and putting it in the forefront of your mind. No matter where you are on the scale of appreciation, you can always bump it up a notch. It's going to be magical when you watch your love life change and grow for the better right in front of your eyes. All it took was a little tweak in your thoughts to the happier, more appreciative side of life.